DISPENSATIONAL DEVELOPMENT AND DEPARTURE

Comparing Classical, Essentialist, and Progressive Dispensational Models

Joseph Parle, Ph.D.

Exegetica Publishing
2020

DISPENSATIONAL DEVELOPMENT AND DEPARTURE:
Comparing Classical, Essentialist, and Progressive Dispensational Models

Written by Joseph Parle, Ph.D

Edited by Catherine Cone, Christiana Cone, and Wisdom Smith
Cover by Abbie Boyd

© 2020 Joseph D. Parle

Published by Exegetica Publishing
Lee's Summit, Missouri

ISBN – 978-0-9982805-6-1

All rights reserved. No part of this publication may be reproduced, stored in a retrieval system, or transmitted in any form or by any means – electronic, mechanical, photocopy, recording, or any other – except for brief quotation in printed reviews, without the prior permission of the publisher.

All Scripture quotations, except those noted otherwise are from the New American Standard Bible,
©1960,1962,1963,1968,1971,1972,1973,1975, 1977, and 1995 by the Lockman Foundation.

This book is dedicated to some very special people in my life. First and foremost, to my Lord and Savior Jesus Christ: thanks for giving me the grace to study your Word. And also, to my beautiful wife who lovingly supported me throughout ministry and studies.

Table of Contents

Chapter 1 – Introduction..1

Chapter 2 – Biographical Sketch of Chafer's Life............................11

Chapter 3 – Chafer's Methodology..31

Chapter 4 – Chafer's Theological System: Soteriology....................61

Chapter 5 – Chafer's Theological System: Sanctification.................87

Chapter 6 – Chafer's Theological System: Israel and the Church....101

Chapter 7 – Chafer's Theological System: Covenants.....................111

Chapter 8 – Chafer's Theological System: Dispensations...............119

Chapter 9 – Chafer's Theological System: Eschatology..................127

Chapter 10 – Chafer's Contributions to Dispensationalism.............135

Postlude..141

Bibliography...143

Acknowledgements

There are many people who deserve acknowledgement for their help on this project, but space only allows for me to acknowledge a few. First, I thank the faculty and staff of Baptist Bible Seminary and Dallas Theological Seminary for accepting me into their program and their help throughout the process. Paul Golden and Barry Phillips were especially helpful in providing hospitality for me throughout all my research in Pennsylvania. I'd like to express appreciation for the late Dr. Robert Lightner. I first read Chafer's *Systematic Theology* in his class at Dallas Theological Seminary. Although I didn't appreciate it then (I thought his writings were too difficult to understand), I'm very thankful that Dr. Lightner exposed us to the original writings of Chafer so we could understand the theology the seminary was built on.

Second, I'd like to thank the College of Biblical Studies. I'd like to thank Dr. William Boyd for allowing me to leave Houston for several weeks during the school year in order to pursue my advanced degrees. I pray that I will make their investment in me pay great dividends. I am also thankful for Dr. Bill Blocker for encouraging me and giving me the time to pursue publication. I also appreciate Dr. Charles Carpenter's assistance with proofreading my work. I also thank Drs. Israel Loken and Steve Sullivan for their guidance. I appreciate Dr. J. B. Hixson's assistance with some of the formatting issues as well as his valuable insight on free grace soteriology.

Third, I'd like to thank my advisors, Drs. Michael Stallard and Kenneth Gardoski, for taking the time to read this work and give me valuable feedback. Dr. Stallard has been especially influential in igniting my passion for systematic theology and historical theology.

Fourth, I'd like to acknowledge my family, especially my wife Suzan. Suzan has been a great source of help and strength for me. I also would like to acknowledge Dr. Dennis and Bertha Parle as well as my parents-in-law Joyce and the late Bernard Seggerman for all of their support throughout the process. I also appreciate my children, Faith and Joe Jr., who have always been patient when I had to work when they wanted me to play. I recognize that I spent a great deal of time studying for this goal and I only hope that it will prove worthwhile to you and God's glory.

Fifth, I am so thankful for Dr. Christopher Cone, Catherine Cone, and Exegetica Publishing for all their help with editing and publishing this work. This project came about a few years ago when I was lamenting to Dr. Cone at the Council on Dispensational Hermeneutics about the paucity of publishers who are willing to publish scholarly dispensational works. I am thankful for his leap of faith in providing this avenue for me.

Finally, I'd like to acknowledge my sincerest appreciation for my Lord and Savior Jesus Christ who is before all things and in Him all things hold together (Colossians 1:17). I hope my life and research will be a holy sacrifice that is acceptable to Him as my spiritual service of worship (Romans 12:1).

1
Introduction

Lewis Sperry Chafer is one of the most misunderstood theologians in the dispensational camp. He is misunderstood by friends and foes of dispensationalism. He is often targeted by progressive dispensationalists for his alleged non-literal approach to hermeneutics. One covenant theologian accused him of being in the "very uncomfortable condition of having two inconsistent systems of religion struggling together in his mind."[1] This book gives a brief historical background on Chafer's life, discusses his theology and evaluates his contributions to dispensationalism. This study particularly emphasizes the continuity between Chafer's form of dispensationalism to essentialist dispensationalism in order to demonstrate that essentialists share more in common than differences with Chafer on key aspects of his theology.

---

[1] Benjamin B. Warfield, "A Review of Lewis Sperry Chafer's 'He That Is Spiritual'," *The Princeton Theological Review* Vol. XVII, (April 1919): 322.

NEED FOR THIS STUDY

Several individuals have already worked to discuss the life and theology of Lewis Sperry Chafer.[2] This work in particular is intended to compare Chafer's ideas with those who claim to be essentialist dispensationalists. One of the key claims of progressive dispensationalists is that there is a marked transition from the classical dispensationalism of Chafer and Darby to the revised dispensationalism of Ryrie and Walvoord. According to progressive dispensationalists, this discontinuity ultimately led to the progressive dispensationalism of Blaising and Bock. This assertion assumes that the distinctions between the three groups are significant enough to warrant different labels. This work reviews Chafer's work in order to see if this book can be sustained.

---

[2] For instance see: Bruce A. Baker, "The Theological Method of Lewis Sperry Chafer," *Journal of Ministry and Theology* 5, no. 1 (Spring 2001): 29–69, Keith H. Essex, "The Preparation and Contributions of Lewis Sperry Chafer" (Th.M. thesis, Dallas Theological Seminary, 1974) 1–73, John D. Hannah, "The Early Years of Lewis Sperry Chafer," *Bibliotheca Sacra* 144, no.573 (January–March 1987): 3–23, George G. Houghton, "Lewis Sperry Chafer, 1871–1952," *Bibliotheca Sacra* 128, (October–December 1971): 291–300, C. F. Lincoln, "Lewis Sperry Chafer," *Bibliotheca Sacra* 109, (October–December 1952): 332–338, and John A. Witmer, "What Hath God Wrought, Fifty Years of Dallas Theological Seminary: Part I: God's Man and His Dream," *Bibliotheca Sacra* 130, (October–December 1973): 291–305.

METHOD FOR THIS STUDY

The primary focus of this study is to concentrate on the life and theology of Lewis Sperry Chafer. As previously mentioned, the purpose is to compare his theology with essentialist dispensationalism. At this juncture, it is important to discuss the terms often used to describe different forms of dispensationalists. One of the key issues of debate is whether there are two forms of dispensationalism or three. Progressive dispensationalists often have three categories: classical dispensationalism, revised dispensationalism, and progressive dispensationalism. Lightner gives a possible motivation for this distinction as follows:

> Progressives are very set on finding various periods within the history of dispensationalism where there have been changes made or developments. They like to talk about the initial period. They like to talk about the classical period and the essentialist or revised period. I personally do not wish to get involved in that kind of breakdown of category. I do not think that is genuine at all. I think that this is an attempt to pave the way for their defense of their own system. What they're really wanting to say is that since dispensationalism has changed from year to year or decade to decade, why get so excited about this new change that we are introducing? Our change is just like the other changes. Dispensationalism has always had various people believing certain things about it within dispensationalism. There has been change; therefore, this is just another one of those changes. However, I do

> not believe the changes are the same at all. To be sure, dispensationalists have always differed, Dr. Walvoord differs at points with Dr. Chafer, Dr. Chafer differs at points with Dr. Ryrie, Dr. Ryrie with Dr. Pentecost, but the core beliefs of dispensationalism *have not changed since Darby* [emphasis his] ... I think that progressive dispensationalists have made this classification of initial, classical, and essential in order to simply argue that there have been these spurts of growth, development, and change; therefore, their view is just another one. I want to categorically reject that thesis because I think there is a world of difference between various differences within the system and altering the foundation of the system. I liken the three essentials, or sine qua non, as the foundation upon which dispensationalism rests. You can't be a dispensationalist without these essentials, in my opinion.[3]

Lightner's overarching concern is that progressive dispensationalism emphasizes discontinuity between classical and revised dispensationalism as part of their overall attempt to justify the changes within their own system.

As a result, Lightner prefers the label *normative dispensationalism*. Lightner states his rationale for using this term as follows:

> In my discussion here, I will use the terms, **normative** [emphasis his], representing what you might call the classic view, and I don't mind the word, *classic*, either.

---

[3] Robert Lightner, "Progressive Dispensationalism," *Conservative Theological Journal* 4, no. 11 (April 2000): 47–49.

They use the term progressive, which implies anything else is nonprogressive. I resent that, therefore, I appeal to Ryrie's term, normative, which implies that theirs is nonnormative. That is exactly what I want to portray, and historically, that is true. It is based in fact. Whether they like it or not or whether it is right or wrong, it certainly is not normative to dispensationalism. Therefore, I will use the terms normative and progressive in my discussion.[4]

Lightner has noted two popular terms for those who prefer two labels for dispensationalism: classic and normative. As a result of assertions like these (i.e. that progressive dispensationalism is not normal) some progressive dispensationalists have taken offense.[5] For this reason, some progressive dispensationalists prefer the label *essentialist dispensationalism*. Bock defines the term as the "approach reflected by Charles C. Ryrie's *Dispensationalism Today* (Chicago, IL: Moody, 1965), with his definition of dispensationalism in terms of the *sine qua non*, whose three elements are a doxological purpose, a literal hermeneutic, and the distinction between Israel and the church."[6] However, as Lightner's comment above already stated, the term progressive dispensationalism can be equally

---

[4] Ibid., 49.
[5] See Bock's discussion of his dislike of the use of the label normative dispensationalist in Darrell L. Bock, "Hermeneutics of Progressive Dispensationalism," in *Three Issues in Contemporary Dispensationalism*, ed. Herbert W. Bateman IV (Grand Rapids, MI: Kregel, 1999), 99–101.
[6] Darrell L. Bock, "The Son of David and the Saints' Task: The Hermeneutics of Initial Fulfillment," *Bibliotheca Sacra* 150, no. 600 (October–December 1993): 440.

judgmental as it implies that all other forms of dispensationalism that are not moving forward are regressive. While Baker acknowledges Bock's approach, he prefers the term *traditional dispensationalist*.[7] Finally, Bock gives the following definition for the progressive dispensationalist label: "'Progressive dispensationalism' focuses on the progress of revelation, so that each subsequent dispensation represents 'progress' in the unified plan of God. This approach argues for more continuity in God's plan than the other categories."[8] With respect to Bock's definition, it must be said that Ryrie's third point emphasizes a great deal of continuity in God's overall doxological purpose. It also emphasizes the progress of revelation.[9] Thus, his definition does not completely address the unique aspects of the progressive dispensationalist system.

While the author of this book personally prefers only two categories of dispensationalism (traditional and progressive), the terms classical, essentialist,[10] and progressive dispensationalism are employed in this work. Having three

---

[7] Bruce A. Baker, "Progressive Dispensationalism & Cessationism: Why They Are Incompatible," *Journal of Ministry and Theology* 8, no. 1 (Spring 2004): 60.

[8] Bock, "The Son of David and the Saints' Task: The Hermeneutics of Initial Fulfillment," 440. This is distinct from Saucy who uses the term "progressive dispensationalism" to distinguish the newer interpretations from the older version of dispensationalism (which he refers to as classical or traditional dispensationalism). See Robert L. Saucy, *The Case for Progressive Dispensationalism: The Interface between Dispensational & Non-Dispensational Theology* (Grand Rapids, MI: Zondervan Publishing House, 1993), 9.

[9] The doxological purpose of God is discussed in more detail on page 81 of this thesis.

[10] When quoting or referring to *Progressive Dispensationalism*, the term *revised* may be used since that is the term that was discussed in that work.

categories, while allowing for more discontinuity between classical and essentialist dispensationalism than the author would prefer, allows for a simpler comparison between Chafer, Ryrie, and Bock. Additionally, the term essentialist seems less apt to cause offense than normative (especially since essentialist is a term that Bock uses). If the author is attempting to employ a word that includes both classical and essentialist dispensationalists (like Ryrie and Chafer for example), the phrase traditional dispensationalist is used.

This book accomplishes its stated purpose by comparing Chafer with a well-known essentialist dispensationalist. The most obvious choice for this comparison is Dr. Charles Ryrie. While others could have been selected (for example, J. Dwight Pentecost, John Walvoord, etc.), Ryrie was selected for several reasons. First, Ryrie is credited with identifying the three essentials that serve as the *sine qua non* of dispensationalism: (1) the separation of the church from Israel, (2) consistent literal interpretation, and (3) the doxological purpose of God. While some have rightly argued that some of these essentials were not only taught by Ryrie,[11] the essentialist label takes its name from those three essentials. Second, both Ryrie and Chafer have a systematic theology that can form a point of comparison. While Ryrie's *Basic Theology* is not as comprehensive as Chafer's eight-volume *Systematic Theology*, there is sufficient similarity in topics to make an adequate

---

[11] See Mike Stallard, "Émile Guers: An Early Darbyite Response to Irvingism and a Precursor to Charles Ryrie," *Conservative Theological Journal* 1, no. 1 (April 1997): 31–46. Stallard rightly argues that Guers did identify the first two points of Ryrie's *sine qua non* of dispensationalism.

comparison.[12] Third, Ryrie is compared to Chafer in dispensationalist writings.

Chafer's and Ryrie's statements are contrasted to perspectives within progressive dispensationalism. While Bock and Blaising are the most prominently evaluated progressive dispensationalists in this work, a wide variety of works and authors are considered. The primary reason for this is that there is no comprehensive systematic theology that has been written by a prominent progressive dispensationalist. Even *Progressive Dispensationalism* does not have an extended treatment of topics such as soteriology and sanctification. Consequently, other articles and books need to be reviewed.

The overall structure of this book is to briefly explore the life of Lewis Sperry Chafer, his methodology, his theological system, as well as his contributions to dispensationalism. In the process of reviewing his theological system, specific comparisons between Chafer, Ryrie, and progressive dispensationalists are made. This book concludes with a summary of the major arguments presented in this work.

LIMITATIONS OF THIS STUDY

In light of this methodology, one should note that a belief by Chafer, Ryrie, Bock, and Blaising should not be interpreted to represent every adherent to their dispensationalist position. There are a wide variety of views

---

[12] Other works by Ryrie and Chafer are consulted because the primary focus of this study is on their systematic theologies, and these books contain an overview of their theological system.

held by all adherents to dispensationalism. However, a comparison of the essential aspects of each author's view is helpful for establishing key differences within each system. Clearly a more ideal approach would be to do a comprehensive survey of every major classical dispensationalist, every major essentialist dispensationalist, as well as every major progressive dispensationalist. This methodology would allow for fewer generalizations but certainly would take much more than the allotted space for this book.

Additionally, the main argument of this book is that there is a great deal of continuity between Chafer and Ryrie while there is discontinuity with progressive dispensationalists. That is all this book is intending to prove. Space does not permit an extensive evaluation of important topics such as progressive dispensationalists' complementary hermeneutic, use of the Old Testament in the New Testament, definition of literal interpretation, analysis of typology, use of second temple literature, or their eschatology. Each of these topics could serve as a topic for a book in and of itself. Instead, this book primarily focuses on areas of agreement and disagreement between classical, essentialist, and progressive dispensationalists. The methodology of both groups are discussed more than the specifics of each position.

2
Biographical Sketch of Chafer's Life

This chapter gives a brief description of Lewis Sperry Chafer's life. It focuses on his early life, his early ministry, his founding of Dallas Theological Seminary, and the latter portion of his life. Particular attention is given to experiences which significantly affected Chafer's theology. This section focuses on the impact of the message of grace in Chafer's conversion, his negative experiences as a music minister with a traveling evangelist, and the significant influence of Scofield on his life.

CHAFER'S EARLY YEARS

Lewis Sperry Chafer was born in Rock Creek, Ohio, on February 27, 1871. His father, Thomas Chafer, was a minister who graduated from Auburn Theological Seminary,[1] and his mother Lomira grew up in the home of a Wesleyan lay preacher.[2] Thomas and Lomira had a passion for music which rubbed off on their son, Lewis. In fact, his father bought Lewis

---

[1] John D. Hannah, "The Early Years of Lewis Sperry Chafer," *Bibliotheca Sacra* 144, no. 573 (January–March 1987): 6.
[2] Keith H. Essex, "The Preparation and Contributions of Lewis Sperry Chafer" (Th.M. thesis, Dallas Theological Seminary, 1974), 7–8.

a silver coronet on his tenth birthday. According to Hannah, they lived in a happy home: "The various letters from this period suggest a buoyant, happy couple, delighting in and well-adjusted to each other and eagerly expecting a ministry in the Congregational church."[3]

Many things changed when Chafer's father died of tuberculosis after Chafer's eleventh birthday.[4] As a result, his mother had to get a job in a local school which allowed the children to complete their elementary education.[5] Lomira supported the family by taking in boarders to their home. Lewis performed odd jobs and studied under Jacob Tuckerman who was the founder of the New Lyme Institute in South New Lyme, Ohio. Hannah summarizes the importance of this time in Chafer's life:

> The four years in South New Lyme were life-shaping for Chafer. First, a deep interest in music as a career was ignited ... Second, Chafer heard an evangelist by the name of Scott preach on the redemptive mercies of Christ ... The sermon on salvation and grace deeply motivated him to be a preacher. In fact, later these doctrines were prominent in his preaching as well as his writings. He became—and should be remembered above all else—as a preacher of the grace of God![6]

Ironically, Scott (the preacher) himself was suffering from tuberculosis at the time and died three weeks after this

---

[3] Hannah, "The Early Years of Lewis Sperry Chafer," 7.
[4] Bruce A. Baker, "The Theological Method of Lewis Sperry Chafer," *Journal of Ministry and Theology* 5, no. 1 (Spring 2001): 37.
[5] Ibid.
[6] Hannah, "The Early Years of Lewis Sperry Chafer," 10.

sermon.[7] Baker states the potential significance of this event, "Whether it was the fact that Scott was obviously suffering from the same disease that took his father, or the overwhelming way in which the subject was presented, it was this sermon that the Holy Spirit used to prompt Lewis to enter full-time ministry."[8]

The precise timing of Chafer's conversion is debated since different biographies provide conflicting information. Green summarizes the issues in the debate well:

> There are a number of debates surrounding this sermon. First, some argue that it was this sermon that resulted in his conversion to Christ. For example, Richards records that Reg Grant quotes Chafer as saying, "I found out later he was dying of tuberculosis. But on that night, I remember sitting on the front row and I heard the words, really heard them for the first time—'by grace are ye saved through faith'—and I put my trust in Christ alone for my salvation. It was as if Scott threw me a flaming torch—the torch of the grace of God—and I've been carrying it ever since." Jeffrey Jon Richards, *The Eschatology of Lewis Sperry Chafer*, 17. This statement concurs with the official record of Dallas Theological Seminary. Others are not so sure, however. Howard wrote, "At seven he had a definite religious crisis, but no one showed any interest in him at the time." "If there had been child evangelism then," he

---

[7] George G. Houghton, "Lewis Sperry Chafer, 1871–1952," *Bibliotheca Sacra* 128, no. 512 (October–December 1971): 292.
[8] Baker, "The Theological Method of Lewis Sperry Chafer," 38.

notes, "they would have landed me high and dry, but people weren't interested in children then and I don't know what happened." Wally Howard, "Accident Man," *Sunday School Promoter* 6 (1944), 19. Similarly, Chafer himself wrote that he was saved at age six in Lewis Sperry Chafer, "Some Facts Concerning My Conversion" *Evangelical Christian* 16 (March 1920), 80 quoted in Hannah, *The Social and Intellectual Origins,* 83–4. It seems best to conclude, as Richards did, "Perhaps the safest route to take is to say whatever experience he did have as a child of seven was confirmed as a youth of thirteen." Ibid. This assumes, of course, that his conversion took place during his father's first pastorate in Rock Creek. Second, there is some debate whether Chafer heard Scott's sermon in the late stages of his time in Rock Creek or in the early days of South New Lyme.[9]

Green provides a very helpful summary of the issues. If Richard accurately recorded the precise words of Chafer, one should give his own testimony the highest weight in the discussion. A childhood conversion would likely correspond to Chafer's free grace soteriology. Perhaps Howard correctly argues that his actual salvation could have been confirmed later in life. At the "Blessings All Mine" annual president's banquet at Gaston Avenue Baptist Church, on March 7, 1952, a person playing his wife Ella Chafer (she had died by this time) described his experience at the age of thirteen when Preacher

---

[9] Robert Green, "Lewis Sperry Chafer and Dallas Theological Seminary," TMs [electronic copy], (Clarks Summit, PA: Baptist Bible Seminary, 2004), 5.

Scott was preaching and "Lewis had never before heard such a clear cut message of salvation by grace ... Preacher Scott dying of tuberculosis, unknowingly dropped his mantle on the thirteen year old farm lad who listened ... and believed."[10] This same play portrays Chafer's wife as saying nothing about a childhood conversion but focuses her discussion on the events that happened when he was thirteen. This would lend credence to the likelihood that Chafer was at least called but probably converted at age thirteen.

In the Spring of 1888, Lewis and his family moved to Oberlin. Once again, his mother took in boarders to provide for her children's education. Chafer studied music in the Oberlin Conservatory of Music from 1889–1891 after spending one year at the preparatory school. Contrary to Richard's statements that Chafer graduated in 1892, Hannah argues that he never completed his undergraduate education there.[11] According to Essex, one significant aspect of the education was that the professors at the music conservatory had a reputation for being chosen for their musical ability as opposed to their piety.[12] Essex describes the effect on Chafer:

> Chafer saw the college moving away from piety while seeing the effects of such a move in the Conservatory, the effect of being trained without spiritual commitment. That is why in later days as president of Dallas Theological Seminary he would make spiritual

---

[10] Lewis Sperry Chafer, *The Lewis Sperry Chafer Papers* (Jamestown, NC: Schnappsburg University Press), microform.
[11] Hannah, "The Early Years of Lewis Sperry Chafer," 11.
[12] Essex, "The Preparation and Contributions of Lewis Sperry Chafer," 13.

life a priority in faculty selection. Oberlin College lost its distinctive theological character and Christian community atmosphere because it bowed to demands that it end its policies of hiring its own graduates. Chafer saw the need for "unity in teaching," and thus hired Dallas Seminary graduates when they were the best prepared men; and he did not bend, like Oberlin College, when criticized for this position.[13]

While Chafer's conversion experience might have provided insights into his soteriology, his experience at Oberlin might have led to his intense interest in living a spiritual life. He witnessed the dangers of neglecting sanctification in the interest of scholarly pursuits at Oberlin and did not want to repeat the same mistake at Dallas Theological Seminary.

This section summarizes the early years of Chafer's life. The most significant events were probably the death of his father, Scott's sermon on grace, and his time at Oberlin. Scott's sermon has particular significance because Chafer describes it as a time when he understood the implications of the relationship between grace and saving faith. This likely contributed to his soteriological beliefs as well as the role grace played in the development of his theological system. His experience at Oberlin likely influenced his focus on the spiritual life in his *Systematic Theology* and at Dallas Theological Seminary.

---

[13] Ibid., 14. This is an interesting departure from the latter practice of some departments to encourage DTS students to get Ph.D. degrees elsewhere in order to enhance the scholarly reputation of the school.

CHAFER'S EARLY MINISTRY

This section discusses Chafer's early ministry. Particular attention is given to his experience as a music minister for Reverend A. T. Reed and his time with C. I. Scofield. This section discusses some of the factors that led Chafer to a greater appreciation for dispensational theology as well as his concern about evangelistic methodology.

Chafer met the Reverend A. T. Reed at a YMCA meeting in 1890 and became his assistant for his evangelistic meetings shortly thereafter.[14] From 1890 to 1896 he attended many meetings and worked with many great evangelists as a result of his involvement with D. L. Moody's tent meetings and revivals. Baker describes the response Chafer had to this ministry experience, "Chafer's previous experience with nationally known evangelistic teams was a considerable disappointment. He strongly disapproved of the high-pressure techniques that were used to induce a decision for Christ."[15] This experience would later contribute to ideas like those he wrote about in *True Evangelism*. In this book, Chafer discusses "the great temptation for the evangelist to be superficial in his aim and undertakings."[16] He was concerned about the poor methodology in which evangelists demanded "some public action in connection with conversion, such as standing or going forward in a meeting."[17] Chafer's concern about connecting

---

[14] Hannah, "The Early Years of Lewis Sperry Chafer," 11.
[15] Baker, "The Theological Method of Lewis Sperry Chafer," 39–40.
[16] Lewis Sperry Chafer, *True Evangelism: Winning Souls by Prayer* (Grand Rapids, MI: Kregel Publications, 1993), 16.
[17] Ibid., 17.

works and salvation would later have a strong impact on his soteriology.

During this time, he also had significant changes in his personal life. He initially met Ella Case at Oberlin. Geiger writes, "He left the farm when he was about eighteen, went to Oberlin College to study music. He was a talented kid, and the profs thought he showed more musical promise than any of the other voice students in his class. Things went fine until that first spring. He couldn't concentrate on his music. He had never daydreamed before. Something was definitely wrong. It was Ella Lorraine Case, his landlady's daughter. And what a coincidence she was a music student too. Dr. Chafer always claimed she came and got him, said he didn't have a chance."[18] They were married on April 22, 1896, in Ellington, New York.

Hannah says that his provider role may have helped in the process of him becoming a preacher: "Several factors converged to put the thought of a musical career behind the Chafers and to thrust him increasingly toward a public preaching ministry. Besides the continuing uncertainty about finances, a lingering thought that God might be directing in a unique way heightened their anxieties."[19] In 1896 Chafer had his first preaching experience and later became a music minister of a local church. Shortly thereafter, Chafer was diagnosed with tuberculosis which was the same disease his father died from. Hannah describes the impact this disease had on his future, "The Chafers interpreted the illness as an indication from the Lord that he should turn toward a preaching ministry, though music would always be a strong component in their work. As soon as the decision was made, his

---

[18] Chafer, *The Lewis Sperry Chafer Papers*.
[19] Hannah, "The Early Years of Lewis Sperry Chafer," 14–15.

distress dissipated, and his doctor marveled at his sudden, complete recovery."[20]

In 1900, Chafer was called to serve as an associate pastor of the First Congregational Church in Buffalo, New York, and he was ordained into the gospel ministry on April 3, 1900.[21] His doctrinal statement for his ordination does not seem to completely coincide with his later theological beliefs. In fact, Green lists three key issues that were distinct from his later beliefs: (1) his belief that the New Covenant was given directly to the church, (2) his apparently amillennial eschatology, and (3) his view of baptism which was consistent with covenant theology.[22]

Chafer's ministry in Buffalo did not last long, and he soon moved to Northfield, Massachusetts. According to Geiger, Chafer wanted to make his headquarters there but was afraid that others would think he was hitching himself to the Northfield name. So, he prayed that if this was God's will he would be invited there, and two days later a letter came from the Northfield Boys' School.[23] Hannah expands on how this time was one of the most significant of Chafer's life:

> This began a period that was to have a very important influence on Chafer's future; there he would meet an array of national and international speakers at the annual Northfield Conferences. Northfield became Chafer's base for his traveling ministry, while he

---

[20] Ibid., 15.
[21] Green, "Lewis Sperry Chafer and Dallas Theological Seminary," 8.
[22] Ibid., 9–10.
[23] Chafer, *The Lewis Sperry Chafer Papers*.

labored there in conference ministry during the summers [footnote: Lewis Chafer to Ella Chafer, December 1902, Keating Summit, Pennsylvania and Ella and Lewis Chafer to Sarah Case, February 11, 1905, Watertown, New York.]. For example, in the winter of 1904 the annual Southland Bible Conference was inaugurated in Crescent City, Florida by H. W. Pope, secretary of Northfield Extension, A. C. Gaebelein of New York, W. R. Moody, George C. Stebbins, and L. C. Chafer [footnote: 61. C. F. Lincoln, "Biographical Summary Sheet," n.d. (unpublished manuscript)] ... In July 1902, apparently in their first summer in Northfield, the Summer School of Bible Study was started with G. Campbell Morgan, W. W. White, George Pentecost, and C. I. Scofield among the teachers [footnote "Northfield Bible School," *Record of Christian Work*, April 1902, p. 296, and "Northfield Bible School," *Record of Christian Work*, August 1902, p. 561. The Bible or Training School was directed by C. I. Scofield, who served as one of the primary instructors ("The Northfield Training School," *Record of Christian Work*, September 1901, p. 669). The curriculum of the school was described in this article as follows: "The whole Bible is covered; and while theology and the great doctrines are taught, these are drawn from the Bible, and expressed in Biblical terms."]. The General Conference of 1903 brought such prominent speakers as W. H. Griffith Thomas, James Orr, R. A. Torrey, G. Campbell Morgan, and A. T. Pierson to the platform with the music directed by George C. Stebbins. The Chafers, among others, blended their baritone and contralto voices in duets [footnote: "The Northfield General Conference for Christian Workers," *Record of Christian Work*, September 1903, pp. 563–68. Cf. also C. F. Lincoln, "Lewis Sperry Chafer: 'Man of God,' " Dallas Theological Seminary, n.d.)]. Though the influence of these speakers on Chafer was significant, the deepest impact seems captured in Witmer's suggestion that "under...their expository teaching of the Bible his own ministry was reoriented from...evangelistic preaching to...Bible exposition [footnote: Witmer, "What God Hath Wrought—Fifty Years of Dallas Theological Seminary," p. 293.]."[24]

Hannah correctly argues that the Northfield conferences gave Chafer significant ministry contacts which would later help shape his ministry. These contacts exposed him to dispensational theology as well as an expositional style of teaching the Bible.

As previously mentioned, Chafer met Cyrus Ingerson Scofield at Northfield. At that time, Scofield was pastor of the Trinitarian Congregational Church of Northfield and director of the Northfield Training School.[25] Houghton describes Scofield's impact on Chafer's call:

> Dr. C. I. Scofield was pastor of the Congregational church in Northfield when the Chafers moved there, and the friendship begun at this time between the two men was to develop into a warm and intimate father-son relationship. Within a few years, after Scofield had

---

[24] Hannah, "The Early Years of Lewis Sperry Chafer," 16–17.
[25] Ibid., 17.

returned to his former pastorate in Dallas, he had Chafer come to the church for special meetings. Scofield impressed upon his friend the value of the Bible teaching gift which he saw in Chafer and urged him to cultivate it. In a long-remembered discussion between the two men, Chafer decided that Scofield's insight was from God.[26]

According to Houghton, Chafer was dedicated to God by Scofield as Chafer knelt by his chair.

One cannot overestimate the impact Scofield had on Chafer's life. Hannah says:

Without dispute the one who had the greatest impact on Chafer in those Northfield days and beyond was Cyrus Ingerson Scofield, then pastor of the Trinitarian Congregational Church of Northfield and director of the Northfield Training School ... Scofield's teaching in the fall of 1901 had a profound influence on Chafer's career and teachings: "Until that time I had never heard a real Bible teacher ... My first hearing of Dr. Scofield was at a morning Bible class at the Bible School. He was teaching the sixth chapter of Romans. I am free to confess that it seemed to me at the close that I had seen more vital truth in God's Word in that one hour than I had seen in all my life before. It was a crisis for me. I was captured for life."[27]

---

[26] Houghton, "Lewis Sperry Chafer, 1871–1952," 293–94.
[27] Hannah, "The Early Years of Lewis Sperry Chafer," 17–18.

Chafer himself said he knew Scofield "as a son may know a father" and that Scofield was "one of the greatest Christians of his generation."[28] Chafer especially appreciated Scofield's intimacy that led "to enjoyment of God and the freedom which enjoyment begets."[29]

From 1906–1909, Chafer taught music and Bible at the Mt. Hermon School for Boys which was founded by D. L. Moody.[30] Chafer's experience teaching Bible caused him to think about the possibility of one day opening a seminary. Witmer says:

> The dream of starting a school for the training of ministers was planted in Dr. Chafer's mind at Northfield. His approachableness and rapport with his students led to many protracted after-class discussions. Many times, some of the boys would accompany him in his carriage a mile or two on his way home, plying him constantly with questions. Some seniors looking forward to preparation for the ministry asked him to consider taking a pastorate in the area and opening his study to them to pursue their ministerial training under him. God did not lead Dr. Chafer to fulfill that request, but it sparked a vision that became incarnate in Dallas Seminary. In the years that followed as Dr. Chafer itinerated in evangelistic and Bible conference ministry, he made a point of quizzing countless pastors concerning areas in which they felt their seminary course of study

---

[28] Lewis Sperry Chafer, "Dr. C. I. Scofield," *Bibliotheca Sacra* 100, no. 397 (January–March 1943): 5.
[29] Ibid.
[30] Hannah, "The Early Years of Lewis Sperry Chafer," 294.

failed to prepare them. Invariably the response was that they were not taught the English Bible in order to be able to minister its truths. The conviction slowly crystallized that a seminary was needed with a distinctive curriculum that would equip men to be expositors of the Word of God. Through these contacts and experiences God prepared Lewis Sperry Chafer for a quarter-century to be His instrument in founding Dallas Theological Seminary.[31]

The experience at the Mt. Hermon School for Boys allowed Chafer to interact with young boys about the Bible. It planted the seeds for the founding of Dallas Theological Seminary.

This section has described the early years of Chafer's ministry. During this time, he got married and entered into music ministry as well as preaching ministry. While leading worship for evangelists, he became concerned about the poor methodology employed. He also got the chance to participate in the Northfield conferences. This introduced him to several key dispensationalists and their expository teaching methodology. He met C. I. Scofield who mentored him and prepared him for ministry. At Mt. Hermon School for Boys he received experience teaching boys theology, which helped plant the seeds for Dallas Theological Seminary.

---

[31] John A. Witmer, "What Hath God Wrought, Fifty Years of Dallas Theological Seminary: Part I: God's Man and His Dream," *Bibliotheca Sacra* 130, no. 520 (October–December 1973): 293–94.

THE FOUNDING OF DALLAS THEOLOGICAL SEMINARY

After working at the Mt. Hermon School for Boys, Chafer began to spend more time with C. I. Scofield. As Scofield became ill, Chafer was given more responsibility in his ministry. This often required Chafer to go to Dallas in order to spend time at Scofield's church which was the First Congregational Church in Dallas. After Scofield's death, in the spring of 1923, Chafer became the pastor of the First Congregational Church in Dallas which was renamed Scofield Memorial Church. At this point in Chafer's life story, it is helpful to briefly explore some of the historical events that led to the founding of Dallas Theological Seminary.

While the Bible conference movement was in full swing, several people thought there was need for additional support. Witmer writes that at a 1923 meeting of the World Christian Fundamentals Association in Fort Worth, Texas, "the conviction was officially expressed that 'one of the greatest needs of the hour...is the establishment of a great evangelical premillennial seminary.'"[32] Witmer summarizes why the need was so great at this time:

> When Dr. Chafer began his ministry, first as a musician and then as an evangelist and Bible teacher, modern religious liberalism and destructive biblical criticism had already made deep inroads into many of the American theological seminaries. The modernist-fundamentalist conflict was beginning in the American denominations. As the social gospel gained acceptance it

---

[32] Ibid., 295.

not only altered the content of the biblical and theological courses in the seminaries but also restructured the curricula by progressively replacing the Bible-oriented materials such as the biblical languages with courses in philosophy, psychology, and sociology. This is at least part of the reason why pastors felt ill-equipped to preach the Word of God to their people.[33]

The school was officially called Evangelical Theological College in April of 1924, and the doctrinal statement was officially adopted by the Board of Trustees March 6, 1925.[34]

From 1924 until his death in 1952, Chafer served as the president of Evangelical Theological College which later became Dallas Theological Seminary. He served as the editor of *Bibliotheca Sacra* and was a professor of systematic theology as well. In a letter entitled "Confidential letter to the Board of Incorporation of the Dallas Theological Seminary" Chafer summarized his presidency as follows:

> During my service as president of the Seminary I have contended for the observance of these particular ideals and have aimed to select men to be associated with me, both officers and faculty, who would share with me in the realization of these ideals. In the main, the objective has been to train men in the exposition of the Sacred Text; not just to preach <u>from</u> the Bible or <u>about</u> [emphasis his] the Bible ... Dallas Seminary aims to prepare men to declare the Scriptures of truth. The realization of this ideal demands a type of discipline

---

[33] Ibid., 294.
[34] Ibid., 299.

quite different and much more extended than the usual Seminary curriculum—especially in the original languages and in the study of the Bible itself. The premillennial, dispensational interpretation is the only one true to the Bible and therefore the only one which opens the Sacred Text to human understanding. All study must be according to this interpretation and much emphasis must be placed on the Spiritual life, for apart from the knowledge of God's ways with His servants the best of training must be useless. It was our so extended and thorough approach to all departments of our work that so easily won the high credit with the University of New York. It has been for me a constant effort to maintain these high standards. The trend will always be down to easier levels. Whoever assumes responsibility after me must not only hold these high standards as ideals, but he must retain them against every opposing influence.[35]

In this quote one can see many aspects of his life that contributed to his philosophy of education at Dallas Theological Seminary. First, his emphasis on expository teaching likely came from what he learned at the Northfield conferences. Second, his desire to instill spiritual life as well as a strong academic environment was likely a result of what he witnessed at Oberlin. For he later says in this same letter, "The Seminary is so unique that for the most part, we have had only failure when employing service men, however highly educated, from

---

[35] Chafer, *The Lewis Sperry Chafer Papers*.

other seminaries. Only a Dallas man will enter the task of maintaining the Dallas standards."[36]

Not only did Chafer lead as president of Dallas Theological Seminary but he also wrote several books as well as his eight-volume *Systematic Theology*. His first published work was *Satan* in 1909.[37] In 1911 he wrote *True Evangelism*. He wrote *The Kingdom in History and Prophecy* in 1915. In 1917 he wrote *Salvation*. He first published *He That Is Spiritual* in 1918. He wrote *Grace* in 1922. In 1926 he wrote *Major Bible Themes*. In 1935 he wrote *The Ephesian Letter*. In 1948, after eleven years of hard work, Chafer finally published his eight-volume *Systematic Theology*. Walvoord stated that this work constituted "a monument in the field of theological literature" since it was "the first consistently premillennial systematic theology ever written."[38] It was an amazing work for its time, and scholars today still benefit from the exceptional insight of the work.

CHAFER'S DEATH

Chafer's wife died in 1944 after a disability that resulted from a stroke.[39] The loss of his wife caused him a great deal of pain. Chafer suffered a heart attack himself in 1935 and a stroke in 1945.[40] In spite of all these challenges, Chafer

---

[36] Ibid.
[37] The dates of Chafer's key works were found in C. F. Lincoln, "Lewis Sperry Chafer," *Bibliotheca Sacra* 109, no. 436 (October–December 1952): 334–35.
[38] John F. Walvoord, "A Review of Lewis Sperry Chafer's 'Systematic Theology'," *Bibliotheca Sacra* 105, no. 417 (January–March 1948): 127.
[39] Baker, "The Theological Method of Lewis Sperry Chafer," 43.
[40] Houghton, "Lewis Sperry Chafer, 1871–1952," 296.

continued to minister after his eightieth birthday.[41] Houghton says regarding Chafer's death, "In the providence of God, Chafer's life of active service for his Lord was to continue until 1952. On August 22 of that year, while in Seattle, Washington, and having suffered further illness, Lewis Sperry Chafer passed into the presence of his Savior."[42] After eighty-one years of teaching about Christ, Chafer finally got to be in His presence. Lynn Landrum said the following in her article entitled "Thinking Out Loud" which was written on August 25, 1952:

> "The Christian is a citizen in heaven," wrote Lewis Sperry Chafer ... "and after he is saved, is detained here in this world in the capacity of a *witness*. He is a *pilgrim and stranger*, an *ambassador* from the court of heaven." Now that Dr. Chafer is dead at eighty-one, no fitter words can be found for inscription on the memorial stone which will most surely be raised in his honor. For such was his citizenship, such was his witness, and such was his embassy among men.[43]

In his last will and testament, Chafer requested that this text be inscribed on his grave marker: "And I will raise him up at the last day (John 6:40)."[44]

---

[41] Baker, "The Theological Method of Lewis Sperry Chafer," 43.
[42] Houghton, "Lewis Sperry Chafer, 1871–1952."
[43] Chafer, *The Lewis Sperry Chafer Papers*.
[44] Ibid.

SUMMARY

This section has reviewed the life of Lewis Sperry Chafer in order to understand the relationship between his life and theology. Chafer's early life introduced him to the gospel of grace. His experience at Oberlin raised his awareness of the dangers of scholarship without piety. His early ministry introduced him to the methodology of many evangelists which influenced his beliefs about the purity of the gospel presentation. His experience at Northfield introduced him to several key individuals who would shape his career as well as their expository teaching style. His time with C. I. Scofield gave him much needed instruction as well as a father figure who could prepare him for ministry. Chafer's experience in developing Dallas Theological Seminary gave him the opportunity to write many important works. One of the most significant works was his *Systematic Theology*. This exceptional work gives great insight into his theological system. Chafer continued to serve as president of Dallas Theological Seminary until 1952 when he died at the age of eighty-one.

3
Chafer's Methodology

This chapter analyzes several aspects of Chafer's methodology. Special attention is given to his view on hermeneutics and interpretive method in comparison to that of essentialist and progressive dispensationalists. This section addresses Chafer's definition of literal interpretation, his view of typology, and his understanding of the relationship between the Old and New Testaments.

SUMMARY OF CHAFER'S METHODOLOGY

Like most dispensationalists, Chafer advocates a literal hermeneutic for interpreting the entire Bible. The outcome of this analysis shows that Chafer defines literal interpretation consistently with essentialist dispensationalists. However, the way he may apply his hermeneutic (especially with respect to typology) varies from how many essentialist dispensationalists interpret today. Nevertheless, this is an important distinction because some progressive dispensationalists appeal to early dispensationalists' use of typology as an argument for discontinuity from the essentialist definition of literal interpretation.¹ Their argument does not suffice because progressive dispensationalists differ in how they *define* and *apply* literal interpretation while Chafer only differs on how he *occasionally applied* literal interpretation.²

LITERAL INTERPRETATION

Chafer's View of Literal Interpretation

This section evaluates Chafer's definition of literal interpretation. Chafer typically uses terms like natural, literal, and grammatical to describe his interpretive method. Thus, Chafer's method has much in common with the historical-grammatical method espoused by essentialist dispensationalists.

For instance, Chafer demonstrates his literal hermeneutical method when he says:

> The prophetic story is largely the fulfillment of the Abrahamic, the Palestinian, and the Davidic Covenants. It includes, also, the realization of the two divine purposes—the earthly purpose centered in Israel and consummated according to Psalm 2:6, and the heavenly purpose centered in the Church and consummated according to Hebrews 2:10. It is here declared with complete assurance that, as prophecies which are now fulfilled were fulfilled in their natural, literal, and

---

[1] See Craig A. Blaising and Darrell L. Bock, *Progressive Dispensationalism* (Wheaton, IL: BridgePoint, 1993), 35.

[2] More often than not, Chafer's way of applying the literal method of interpretation has much more in common with an essentialist approach than a progressive one. This book evaluates what overarching presuppositions about typology affected the way he analyzed types.

grammatical meaning, in like manner all that remains—reaching to eternal ages—will be fulfilled in the natural, literal, and grammatical way which the predictions imply. None could question with fairness that the prophecy now fulfilled has followed the literal method to the last detail. It is therefore both unreasonable and unbelieving to suppose that, to relieve some incredulity, the predictions yet unfulfilled will be realized in some spiritualized manner.[3]

This quote indicates several important issues. First, Chafer uses "natural," "literal," and "grammatical" as the key ways of describing his interpretive method. Second, the scope of literal interpretation encompasses the entire Bible. Chafer discusses the literal interpretation of the Old Testament covenants, past prophecies, and future prophecies. Thus, Chafer argues on the basis of past fulfilled prophecies that the entire Bible should be interpreted literally: "There could be no more decisive reason for giving a literal interpretation to the prophecies of the second advent than is set up by the fact that the prophecies of the first advent were thus fulfilled. Those who persist in a change of plan for the interpretation of that which is future have assigned to themselves the unenviable task of explaining why so violent a variation is introduced."[4]

---

[3] Lewis Sperry Chafer, *Systematic Theology*, vol. 4, *Ecclesiology, Eschatology* (Grand Rapids, MI: Kregel Publications, 1993), 288.
[4] Lewis Sperry Chafer, *Systematic Theology*, vol. 5, *Christology* (Grand Rapids, MI: Kregel Publications, 1993), 281.

Ryrie's View of Literal Interpretation

Chafer's definition of literal interpretation is similar to an essentialist definition. Ryrie's famous definition of literal as "clear, plain, and normal" is reflected in his definition of literal which he says is "to interpret plainly one must first of all understand what each word means in its normal grammatical historical sense."[5] Chafer advocates this definition of literal interpretation, and he applies it to the entire Bible.

Not only does Ryrie define literal interpretation, but he also considers it essential to the dispensational system. He considers literal interpretation to be a *sine qua non* of dispensationalism. According to Ryrie, "All conservatives, whatever their eschatological persuasions, use literal or normal interpretation everywhere except eschatology."[6] In Ryrie's view, the amillennialist interpreter puts far more limitations on literal interpretation than figurative interpretation.[7] According to Ryrie, some of these limitations on literal interpretation include the following:

> (a) the presence of figures of speech that cannot be interpreted literally allows us freedom to interpret in other ways; (b) the fact that the main theme of the Bible is spiritual gives validity to figurative or spiritual interpretation; and (c) the fact that the Old Testament is preliminary and preparatory to the New Testament causes us to expect that the New Testament will

---

[5] Charles Caldwell Ryrie, *A Survey of Bible Doctrine* (Chicago, IL: Moody Press, 1995), 48.
[6] Charles Caldwell Ryrie, *Basic Theology*, 517.
[7] Ibid.

interpret the literal Old Testament prophecies in a figurative manner.[8]

In contrast to the amillennialist, Ryrie argues that the premillennialist employs "a literal or normal hermeneutic. And this, of course, gives their picture of future events."[9] Thus, Ryrie considers the chief distinction for dispensational premillennialism to be the consistent literal approach in all areas including eschatology.

Blaising and Bock's View of Literal Interpretation

Blaising and Bock argue that Ryrie's definition of literal interpretation as clear, plain, and normal interpretation was prior to several advancements in scholarly research. As a result, Blaising and Bock prefer to substitute the phrase grammatical-historical for literal or the clear, plain, and normal interpretation. They argue that classical dispensationalism cannot claim to employ this method "since they did not seek to practice such a hermeneutic consistently or exclusively."[10] This statement does not accurately reflect the circumstances. As the following discussion shows, the clear intent of classical dispensationalists like Chafer was to employ a literal hermeneutic. The only exception was when they employed typology because of their assumption that the entire Old Testament prophetically pointed to Christ. However, their intent was to limit the use of typology as much as possible. Thus, one cannot dismiss the essential nature of literal interpretation to dispensationalism based on this practice.

---

[8] Ibid.
[9] Charles Caldwell Ryrie, *Basic Theology*, 523.
[10] Blaising and Bock, *Progressive Dispensationalism*, 37.

Progressive dispensationalists also believe that historical-grammatical interpretation is preferable to the term literal, because not even revised dispensationalists apply it consistently. They also argue that "consistently grammatical-historical interpretation, in the sense in which grammatical-historical is meant today, is much closer to being realized in the hermeneutics of progressive dispensationalism."[11]

Blaising and Bock point to possible risks when employing literal interpretation. However, one must question whether the possibility of abuse would require a change in terminology. Bock and Blaising consistently use the same term with different definitions. As a result, their historical-grammatical view is significantly dissimilar to Chafer's and Ryrie's.

HERMENEUTICS

Chafer's Hermeneutical System

In addition to his definition of literal interpretation, one must explore Chafer's overall hermeneutical system. This includes his definition of hermeneutics and the methodology he employs. This discussion demonstrates that neither Chafer's definition nor his proposed methodology differs substantially from an essentialist approach.

Chafer defines hermeneutics as follows:

The doctrine of interpretation contemplates the science of discovering the exact meaning of the Spirit Author as

---
[11] Ibid.

> this is set forth in a given Scripture passage. Such a science may be described theologically as *hermeneutics*. To fathom this doctrine it is necessary to know and follow the recognized rules of Scripture interpretation.[12]

This quotation demonstrates several aspects of Chafer's hermeneutical theory. First, he believes hermeneutics is a science. Second, he relates it to interpretation which has its goal as precisely discovering the divine Author's intended meaning of the Scripture. These aspects of his definition of hermeneutics are consistent with the essentialist definition.

Chafer states the consequences of employing poor hermeneutical methodology in the following way:

> It is exceedingly easy to twist or mold the Word of God to make it conform to one's preconceived notions. To do this is no less than "handling the word of God deceitfully" (2 Cor. 4:2), and is worthy of judgment from Him whose Word is thus perverted. At no point may the conscience be more exercised and the mind of God more sought than when delving into the precise meaning of the Scriptures and when giving those findings to others.[13]

---

[12] Lewis Sperry Chafer, *Systematic Theology*, vol. 7, *Doctrinal Summarization* (Grand Rapids, MI: Kregel Publications, 1993), 203.
[13] Lewis Sperry Chafer, *Systematic Theology*, vol. 1, *Prolegomena, Bibliology, Theology Proper* (Grand Rapids, MI: Kregel Publications, 1993), 119.

Chafer had significant concerns about theologians who eisegetically tried to twist verses in the Bible to conform with their preconceived notions.

Lewis Sperry Chafer believed that one must incorporate the right methods in hermeneutical interpretation. In his *Systematic Theology*, Chafer primarily quotes from Rollin T. Chafer's four rules for Bible Interpretation.[14] Rollin Chafer's first guideline deals primarily with the interpretation of individual words. The key aspect of this guideline is finding the singular meaning of the word as intended by the original author:

> The first rule of Biblical interpretation is: Interpret grammatically; with due regard to the meaning of words, the form of sentences, and the peculiarities of idiom in the language employed. The sense of Scripture is to be determined by the words; a *true* knowledge of the words is the knowledge of the sense ... The words of Scripture must be taken in their common meaning, unless such meaning is shown to be inconsistent with other words in the sentence, with the argument or context, or with other parts of Scripture ... The true meaning of any passage of Scripture, then, is not every sense which the words will bear, nor is it every sense which is true in itself, but that which is intended by the

---

[14] Surprisingly, most of the doctrinal summary on interpretation in Chafer's *Systematic Theology*, volume 7, pages 203–205, is a very large quote of Rollin Chafer's textbook called *The Science of Biblical Hermeneutics*.

inspired writers, or even by the Holy Spirit, though imperfectly understood by the writers themselves.[15]

Once again, this guideline shows the necessity of the historical-grammatical interpretation method for interpreting a word contextually.

The second rule deals with the larger context. Lewis Sperry Chafer quotes his brother Rollin T. Chafer on the second rule which is to "interpret according to the context."[16] Rollin T. Chafer concludes, "The study of the context is the most legitimate, efficacious, and trustworthy resource at the command of the interpreter. Nothing can be more convenient, more logical than to explain an author by himself, and to have recourse to the entire train of thought."[17]

The third rule deals with the overall purpose of the book. One can still note the overall progression that Rollin Chafer developed from the smaller parts to the larger whole. Rollin Chafer writes:

> Sometimes the context does not give all the light needed to determine the meaning of a word or a phrase ... The purpose in writing a book is often clearly mentioned, especially in the N.T. Epistles. This avowed purpose will often throw light on passages otherwise obscure."[18]

Thus, Chafer believed that an individual passage should be interpreted in light of the overall purpose of the author.

---

[15] Ibid., vol. 7, 203–4.
[16] Ibid., 204.
[17] Ibid., 205.
[18] Ibid.

The fourth interpretive rule employed by Rollin T. and Lewis Sperry Chafer deals with the analogy of faith. Rollin Chafer says:

> The fourth and most comprehensive rule of Biblical interpretation is: Compare Scripture with Scripture ... A Scripture truth is really the consistent explanation of all that Scripture teaches in reference to the question examined; and a Scripture duty is the consistent explanation of all the precepts of Scripture on the duty (Angus–Green, *op. cit.*, p. 195). As has already been noted, this procedure was not employed until the Reformation; and sound hermeneutics was not developed until this method was adopted. It results in "the analogy of faith which regulates the interpretation of each passage in conformity with the whole tenor of revealed truth."[19]

This aspect of Chafer's hermeneutical method deals with interpreting the Bible in light of the larger whole. Note that in Chafer's system this did not trump the results of steps one through three as it sometimes does with some Reformed scholars. Rollin T. and Lewis Sperry Chafer believed that the right literal methodology would produce the right results.

Ryrie's Hermeneutical System

Once again, there are strong similarities between the essentialist view and Rollin Chafer's (and by implication Lewis Sperry Chafer's since Rollin Chafer's hermeneutical principles

---

[19] Ibid.

were quoted directly in Lewis Sperry Chafer's *Systematic Theology*). Like Chafer, Ryrie defines hermeneutics as "The study of the principles of interpretation."[20] Ryrie lists four basic principles of literal interpretation in his *Basic Theology*: (1) interpret grammatically, (2) interpret contextually, (3) compare Scripture with Scripture, and (4) recognize the progressiveness of revelation.[21] This once again demonstrates continuity between Chafer's hermeneutics and literal interpretation as opposed to discontinuity. It is also important to note that Chafer and Ryrie not only agree on the definition of literal interpretation but also on the extent to which it should be applied, that is the entire Bible.

Blaising and Bock's Hermeneutical System

While there is a great deal of continuity between the method of Chafer and Ryrie, there is discontinuity with the method of Bock and Blaising. As opposed to the traditional historical-grammatical method of interpretation, they espouse a historical-grammatical-literary-theological method. This is a significant shift from the classical and essentialist dispensational method to the progressive dispensational method.

As previously mentioned, Blaising and Bock believe that the traditional literal or clear, plain, and normal view of interpretation is somewhat outdated. Since this method was developed, scholarship has identified several aspects of interpretation that must be incorporated in the process.

---

[20] Charles Caldwell Ryrie, *Basic Theology: A Popular Systemic Guide to Understanding Biblical Truth* (Chicago, IL: Moody Press, 1999), 627.
[21] Ibid., 129.

Consequently, they suggest the historical-grammatical-literary-theological approach as the appropriate method. They believe that this "fourfold description of hermeneutics is really what most mean when they speak simply of the historical-grammatical method."[22] Once again Blaising and Bock use the same term as traditional and essentialist dispensationalists but with a different meaning. One must seek to understand what they mean by "most" people who imply a fourfold nature of hermeneutics. Certainly, Ryrie and Chafer do not fall into this category as do most classical and essentialist dispensationalists. Ryrie seems to distinguish literal interpretation from theological interpretation (one of the fourfold aspects that Bock and Blaising employ) when he writes, "The consistent use of literal interpretation leads to a distinction between Israel and the church, while theological interpretation does not."[23]

In contrast to Chafer and Ryrie, Bock and Blaising define the historical approach as that "which seeks to be sensitive to the message as it came to the initial audience, understanding original terms and ideas."[24] They define the grammatical approach as "how the terminology of that message is laid out."[25] According to Bock and Blaising, this is necessary because terms cannot be understood in isolation from each other. Third, they define the need for the literary theological approach based on their belief that "there is an abiding message and unity in the text, which is laid out literarily in

---

[22] Blaising and Bock, *Progressive Dispensationalism*, 77.
[23] Ryrie, *Basic Theology*, 128.
[24] Blaising and Bock, *Progressive Dispensationalism*, 77.
[25] Ibid.

various ways called genres."²⁶ They also believe that the interpreter must consider "the changing nature of the terrain within the text, as well as an appreciation of the various angles to present the truth."²⁷

Additionally, Bock and Blaising argue that a text can have multiple meanings. They confuse interpretation and application. One can even note that their title for chapter two on hermeneutics is "Interpreting the Bible-How We Read Texts" and their title for chapter three is called "Interpreting the Bible-How the Texts Speak to Us." They utilize Hirsch's concepts of meaning and significance but argue that "textual meaning is not really limited to reproducing what the reader thinks the author might have meant."²⁸

USE OF TYPOLOGICAL INTERPRETATION

Chafer's View and Use of Typological Interpretation

One of the most criticized aspects of Chafer's hermeneutical method is his excessive identification of types. This is not consistent with his previously stated rules of interpretation. This inconsistency is primarily due to some presuppositions he had about typology in the Old Testament. This section describes his rules for typology and evaluate his application of those rules within his writing. To begin with, Chafer defines a type as follows:

> A type is a divinely purposed anticipation which illustrates its antitype. These two parts of one theme are

---

[26] Ibid.
[27] Ibid.
[28] Ibid., 64.

> related to each other by the fact that the same truth or principle is embodied in each. It is not the prerogative of the type to establish the truth of a doctrine; it rather enhances the force of the truth as set forth in the antitype. On the other hand, the antitype serves to lift its type out of the commonplace into that which is inexhaustible and to invest it with riches and treasures hitherto unrevealed.[29]

According to Chafer, a type could be a person, an event (for example, the Exodus, the passage through the Red Sea, etc.), a thing of some kind (for example, the tabernacle, the laver, the lamb of sacrifice, etc.), an institution (for example, the Sabbath, animal sacrifice, Melchizedekian priesthood, David's kingdom), or a ceremony which he considers to be "all Old Testament appointments for the service of God."[30]

Chafer expresses concerns about potential abuses of typology when he writes:

> Typology, like prophecy, has often suffered more from its friends than its foes. The fact that extremists have failed to distinguish between that which is typical and that which is merely allegorical, analogous, parallel, happy illustration, or resemblance, may have driven conservative theologians from the field. When truth is tortured by faddists and extremists, an added obligation is thereby imposed upon conservative scholarship to declare it in its right proportions. It is obvious that to neglect truth is a greater error than to overemphasize it

---

[29] Chafer, *Systematic Theology*, vol. 1, xxx.
[30] Ibid., vol. 7, 308.

or to misstate it; and typology, though abused by some, is, nevertheless, conspicuous by its absence from works on Systematic Theology.[31]

This quotation expresses two possible extremes that Chafer was concerned about: excessive attention to typology and neglect of typology in systematic theology. In order to avoid both extremes, Chafer sets the following guidelines for typology:

> a. Types are found in the Old Testament, and there mostly in the Pentateuch; they cover the wide range of truth and subjects named above.
> b. Strictly speaking, a type is that which has been so indicated in the Bible. 1 Corinthians 10:11, however, is of great import in this connection.
> c. Types are one of three binding factors to link together the two Testaments: (1) types, (2) prophecies, and (3) continuity of truth.
> d. Types are predictions because they foreshadow what was future at the time of the Old Testament.
> e. Types are as much inspired as any of the Scriptures and are intended of God for either admonition or instruction.
> f. Christ is the outstanding antitype in all typology.[32]

Most essentialist dispensationalists would agree with the limitation of typology to that which is found in the Bible as per point "b." However, many essentialist dispensationalists would

---

[31] Ibid., vol. 1, xxix–xxx.
[32] Ibid., vol. 7, 309.

disagree with Chafer's application of these rules in specific instances. One of the most significant abuses of typologies in Chafer's writings is his presupposition of the links of Old Testament brides with the church:

> Of the various unions of the Old Testament which men have defended as being typical of the Church in her relation to Christ, only two will be considered at any length here. It is reasonable to suppose that when an account is given of the marriage of any man of the Old Testament who is himself a type of Christ, that marriage may have typical signification. Moses is a type of Christ as Deliverer; thus, Zipporah, his wife, taken from the Gentiles while he was away from his brethren, is a suggestion of the calling out of the Church during the period between the two advents of Christ. David is a type of Christ, and, of all his wives, Abigail serves best to illustrate the true Bride. She left all to be joined to David. Boaz, too, is a type of Christ as Kinsman Redeemer; and Ruth, the poor Moabitess, discovering that Boaz would not rest until he had finished the redemption which would place her as coinheritor of all his position and wealth, gave herself to him as the one beloved.[33]

The major problem with Chafer's use of typology here is not his methodology but the driving assumption that causes him to violate the rules he already set for typology. In the previous quote Chafer argues that it is "reasonable to suppose" that the wife of a type of Christ may relate to the church without any

---

[33] Ibid., vol. 4, 137.

Biblical support for doing so. Thus, one cannot argue that Chafer was not literal in his approach to interpretation. Instead, he advocates a literal means of interpretation, but he might consider some passages of the Bible to be typological even though the Bible does not specifically claim something was a type. This was primarily due to his presuppositions about the typological significance of brides of types of Christ in the Bible.

Ryrie's View of Typology Compared with Chafer's

In contrast to Chafer, Ryrie says far less about typology in *Basic Theology*. This is probably because Ryrie did not share the assumption of Gaebelein and Chafer that much of the Old Testament may prophetically point to Christ.[34] Instead, Ryrie discusses typology within the context of the literal, historical grammatical method. For instance, he writes:

> Remember that when symbols, parables, types, etc. are used, they depend on an underlying literal sense for their very existence, and their interpretation must always be controlled by the concept that God communicates in a normal, plain, or literal manner. Ignoring this will result in the same kind of confused exegesis that characterized the patristic and medieval interpreters.[35]

---

[34] For a description of Gaebelein's belief that all Biblical history is prophetic see Michael D. Stallard, *The Early Twentieth-Century Dispensationalism of Arno C. Gaebelein* (Lewiston, NY: The Edwin Mellon Press, 2002), 170–74.
[35] Ryrie, *Basic Theology*, 17.

Ryrie speaks of typology in a much more limited sense. He argues that God's clear communication would not make hidden messages in the Old Testament very likely.

There is significant difference between Ryrie and Chafer's use of typology. However, this area is not so significant in and of itself to warrant different labels for each group or to argue that progressive dispensationalism is continuing the process of change started by essentialist dispensationalism.

Bock and Blaising's View of Typology Compared with Chafer

Bock and Blaising argue for significant distinctions in their use of typology as opposed to the classical and essentialist perspective. They mainly believe that the purpose for which typology is employed is distinct. This section reviews the assertions they make in comparison with Chafer. Bock and Blaising address the topic of typology in *Progressive Dispensationalism* when they write:

> Progressive dispensationalists view typology as an aspect of historical-literary interpretation. This is not the same kind of typology as practiced in classical dispensationalism. The latter was oftentimes a form of "spiritual interpretation" in which material objects, persons, or other phenomena represented something in the spiritual world. For example, oil was thought to be a "type" of the Holy Spirit, and leaven was considered a "type" of evil. In contrast to this, typology in historical-literary hermeneutics refers to patterns of resemblance between persons and events in earlier history to persons and events in later history. For example, the Davidic-

Solomon kingdom is a type of the eschatological kingdom, the Day of the Lord judgment in the sixth century B.C. is a type of the future, eschatological Day of the Lord. Consequently, typology for progressive dispensationalism is primarily a "horizontal" (historical) relationship rather than a "vertical" (spiritual) one.[36]

The contrast between progressive dispensationalism and classical dispensationalism (represented by Chafer, Gaebelein, and Darby) is a fair one. Bock and Blaising are correct that they use typology differently. Classical dispensationalists used it because of their assumption that much of the Old Testament prophetically pointed to Christ. However, they interpreted prophecy literally. Progressive dispensationalists tend to interpret much of the Old Testament literally but sometimes interpret the covenants and prophecy typologically.

Both of these approaches differ substantially from the essentialist view of typology. Blaising and Bock acknowledge:

> However, they [revised dispensationalists] differed from classical dispensationalists in their gradual withdrawal from "typology," the spiritual hermeneutic of the earlier dispensationalists. Revised dispensationalists claimed to follow *only* a literal interpretation of Scripture, and the results of such an interpretation would yield dispensationalism (that is *revised* dispensationalism).[37]

This comment does clearly delineate a difference between progressive dispensationalists, classical dispensationalists, and

---

[36] Blaising and Bock, *Progressive Dispensationalism*, 52–53.
[37] Ibid., 35.

revised dispensationalists. Thus, with respect to typology, there is discontinuity in how each group employs it. Classical dispensationalists used it to find prophetic meanings in the Old Testament narrative that point to Christ. Progressives utilize typology as a pattern of resemblance in the historical view of Scripture. Essentialist dispensationalists generally only use typology when the Bible specifically calls something a type.[38]

THE USE OF THE OLD TESTAMENT IN THE NEW TESTAMENT

Chafer's View of the Use of the Old Testament in the New Testament

The debate over the use of the Old Testament in the New Testament among dispensationalists was not nearly as intense in Chafer's era as it is in the current era of the history of dispensationalism. The essentialist dispensationalist will not find precise statements on the rules governing the use of the Old Testament in the New Testament in Chafer's system as one would expect in a current dispensational systematic theology. Chafer describes the relationship between the Old

---

[38] There is some disagreement about this among essentialist dispensationalists. Some only argue for a type when the Bible specifically calls something a type or makes strong connections in this regard (cf. Romans 5:14; Hebrews 11:19). Some allow for additional types when there is strong textual support. For example, essentialist dispensationalists may disagree about whether Joseph is a type for Christ. Those who specifically limit typology to Scriptural indicators would not. Those who argue that strong similarities determine a type would. Either way, most essentialist dispensationalists would not employ typology in the same way classical and progressive dispensationalists do.

Testament and New Testament in his writings instead of an analysis of the exegetical methods that the New Testament writers used when quoting from the Old Testament.

Chafer's primary concern with the relationship between the New and Old Testament was related to prophetic interpretation. Chafer believed that one of the primary reasons the Old Testament was misapplied to the church was due to the failure to study prophecy:

> The entire Old Testament expectation is involved with its earthly kingdom, the glory of Israel, the promised Messiah seated on David's throne in Jerusalem. When these are applied to the Church, as too often they are, there is not so much as an accidental similarity on which to base that application. It may be well restated that such incongruity in doctrine as is developed by confusing Judaism with Christianity can exist only because of the failure to consider the issues involved. This is not to charge opponents with dishonesty; it is rather to call attention to their failure, as pointed out before, to study these great themes. This failure is clearly exposed in the fact that such schools of interpretation have never produced a constructive literature bearing on prophecy.[39]

In Chafer's opinion, this failure to study Old Testament prophecy caused interpreters to miss the continuity of the Old and New Testament. Chafer believed that the means of interpreting both testaments was basically the same:

---

[39] Lewis Sperry Chafer, "An Introduction to the Study of Prophecy," *Bibliotheca Sacra* 100, no. 397 (January–March 1943): 109.

> There is no proper approach to the Synoptic Gospels other than to see them as the fulfillment of the Old Testament prediction respecting the Messiah. Similarly, the book of Revelation is the terminal, like trunk lines running into a union station, of the highways of Biblical prophecy. The Bible presupposes that the reader, when reaching the last book of the Bible, will have in mind all that has gone before; and, to the same degree, these highways of prophecy are incomplete until traced to their end in that incomparable prophetic book. This serves to emphasize the truth that the whole Bible in all its parts is an interrelated and interdependent message, and that the student who does not have as clear a grasp of prophecy as he has of other features of revelation is, by so much, disqualified to interpret any portion of the Word of God.[40]

Chafer emphasized continuity in the message of the Bible and not necessarily an artificial unity of a covenant of grace to one people of God.

Chafer believed that the New Testament basically added information to the prophetic message of the Old Testament; it did not replace the original message to the original audience:

> The Old Testament having closed without realization of the presence of the Messiah or of Israel's kingdom, the New Testament opens with the appearance of the King and the offer to Israel of her long-predicted kingdom (cf.

---

[40] Ibid., 104.

Matthew 1:1; 2:1-2; 4:17; Romans 15:8). The same records go on to declare the rejection of the King and His Kingdom (Matthew 23:37-38) and indicate that all these divine purposes will be fulfilled without failure when the King returns. Certain new themes of prophecy are introduced in the New Testament in addition to the continuing unto consummation of Old Testament themes. The major New Testament themes are: (1) the new age, (2) the new divine purpose, (3) the nation Israel, (4) the Gentiles, (5) the great tribulation, (6) Satan and the forces of evil, (7) the second coming of Christ, (8) the Messianic kingdom, and (9) the eternal state.[41]

Rather than believing in two separate messages, Chafer emphasized continuity. The New Testament builds on the prophetic foundation that was set in the Old Testament; it does not replace it. As a result, Chafer interpreted the Old Testament literally and then synthesized it with the New Testament.

Ryrie's View of the Use of the Old Testament in the New Testament Compared with Chafer's

Ryrie addresses the use of the Old Testament in the New Testament. Like essentialist dispensationalists, he does not believe that the use of the Old Testament in the New Testament gives sufficient reason to invalidate literal interpretation of the Bible. He does so on the basis of the relatively small number of non-literal interpretations as well

---

[41] Chafer, *Systematic Theology*, vol. 4, 385.

as the lack of apostolic authority to interpret the Bible non-literally. For instance, he writes:

> The most frequent objection by evangelicals to normal interpretation points out that since the New Testament uses the Old Testament in a nonliteral sense, we also may interpret Old Testament prophecies (about the Millennium, for example) in a nonliteral sense. Or to put it more simply: since the New Testament spiritualizes the Old Testament, so can we.
>
> This might seem at first glance to be a strong objection to the consistent use of normal hermeneutics. However, we must remember that most often the New Testament uses the Old Testament prophecies literally and does not spiritualize them. Instances cited where the New Testament uses a nonliteral hermeneutic in relation to Old Testament prophecies number only seven at most. Other uses of the Old Testament include using it (a) illustratively (Romans 9:9–12); (b) analogically (1 Corinthians 1:19); (c) applicationally (Romans 12:19); (d) rhetorically (James 4:6); but (e) usually as fulfilled directly, eschatologically, or typically (Acts 2:25–29; John 13:18).
>
> Hardly ever do New Testament writers not use the Old Testament in a historical-grammatical sense (which, of course, includes the use of figures of speech). The rule is that they interpreted the Old Testament plainly; exceptions are rare and typological (but in a sense all of the Old Testament is typical in relation to the fuller revelation of the New Testament).

However, the crux of the matter is this: Can we as interpreters follow the example of the biblical writers in these rare exceptional uses of the Old Testament that seem to be nonliteral? Of course, the answer is yes, if we want to. But if we do it, we do so without apostolic authority, only with personal authority; comparatively, that is not much authority. Any and all uses of the Old Testament that the New Testament writers made were made under divine inspiration and were therefore done properly and authoritatively. If we depart from the plain sense of the text, we do so improperly without such authority. What the biblical writers wrote was infallible; the work of all interpreters is fallible.[42]

Ryrie addresses this issue in a much more detailed sense than Chafer. However, Chafer probably would not have necessarily disagreed with the principles Ryrie espouses. While Chafer argues for typology in the Old Testament, he certainly does not believe that the use of the Old Testament in the New Testament allows one to dismiss the literal interpretation of the Bible.

Bock's View of the Use of the Old Testament in the New Testament Compared with Chafer's

Bock addresses his views in his two-part series entitled "Evangelicals and the Use of the Old Testament in the New."[43]

---

[42] Ryrie, *Basic Theology*, 130.
[43] See Darrell L. Bock, "Part 1: Evangelicals and the Use of the Old Testament in the New," *Bibliotheca Sacra* 142, no. 567 (July–September 1985): 209–24. Also consult Darrell L. Bock, "Part 2: Evangelicals and the Use of the Old Testament in the New," *Bibliotheca Sacra* 142, no. 568 (October–December 1985): 306–19.

There is a tendency in Bock's methodology to try to identify a compromise between competing views. Additionally, his approach is dissimilar to Ryrie's and Chafer's.

To begin with, Bock elaborates on his methodology in analyzing this issue in part one of his article. His basic approach is to summarize the competing views on this topic and give his input on them. After this task is completed, he hopes to do the following:

> Also, a framework for dealing with the Old Testament in the New will be presented that reflects consideration of these key hermeneutical issues and draws from the contributions of each of these schools. Hopefully this two-part discussion will lead to a better understanding of the debate in this complex area and will provide a basis for better dialogue. It is also hoped that the proposed framework in the second article can serve as a functional working model for a way to approach the subject of the Old Testament in the New.[44]

Progressive dispensationalists tend to try to find a mediating position among competing views. This is not inherently a bad thing. Dialogue among individuals with competing theologies is important. However, unlike Ryrie and Chafer, their approach seems to start with competing views first and their analysis of Scripture comes second. Chafer and Ryrie tend to begin with the terminology, followed by an analysis of the key passages, and then followed by interaction with competing views. The order of this approach might lead to different results.

---

[44] Bock, "Part 1: Evangelicals and the Use of the Old Testament in the New," 210.

After interacting with several views (including those of essentialist dispensationalist Elliott Johnson), Bock comes to the following conclusion:

> The theses of this article are four: (1) A distinction between divine intention and the intent of the human author is to be made; but both intentions are related in their basic meaning and that relationship can be articulated. (2) Meaning involves the sense of a passage and not primarily the referents of a passage; but the language of an Old Testament passage and its New Testament fulfillment can be related in terms of referents in one of several ways. (3) The progress of revelation affects the detailed understanding of Old Testament passages in specifying details about the completion of the promise and the completion of salvific patterns in God's revelation. But one should always be aware of (a) what was originally understood by the human author at the time of the original revelation and (b) what God disclosed about the details of that revelation through later revelation or through events in Jesus' life. (4) New Testament alterations of Old Testament texts were neither arbitrary changes to create fulfillment in the New Testament nor reflections of later church theology placed back anachronistically into the lips of Jesus or the early church; rather they reflect accurate Biblical theological considerations of the New Testament authors on the original Old Testament text.[45]

---

[45] Bock, "Part 2: Evangelicals and the Use of the Old Testament in the New," 315–16.

Thus, from Bock's perspective, the focus should not only be on the literal interpretation of the passage at the time of the writing that is reflected in the intent of the human author but the overall intent of the Divine Author. Bock rejects a "total" identification between the divine intent and the human author's intent because "in certain Psalms, as well as in other Old Testament passages, theological revelation had not yet developed to the point where the full thrust of God's intention was capable of being understood by the human author."[46] As a result, the distinction between the intention of the human author and the intent of the Divine Author requires a different interpretive technique.

One can observe several key distinctions between Bock and Ryrie.[47] Ryrie begins with the majority of Biblical evidence and then tries to conform the exceptions to the majority. While he interacts with other views, his main intention is to evaluate which position is most consistent with the record presented in Scripture. Furthermore, he tends to focus more intently on the literal interpretation of the passage and the singularity of meaning in his approach. Bock tends to focus on the progress of revelation and the synthesis of the entire Bible, while Ryrie focuses more on the immediate context and original audience of the passage for defining the meaning.[48]

---

[46] Bock, "Part 2: Evangelicals and the Use of the Old Testament in the New," 309.

[47] Chafer did not speak extensively on the topic since it was likely less controversial when he wrote his *Systematic Theology*.

[48] For more information on an essentialist view of the theological method of literal interpretation in light of the relationship between the Old Testament and New Testament see Mike Stallard, "Literal Interpretation, Theological Method, and the Essence of

CHAPTER SUMMARY

This chapter compares the method of Chafer with Ryrie's. One can note from this discussion that there is a great deal of continuity between Chafer and Ryrie with respect to method. They both employ the historical grammatical method of exegesis. They both focus on literal interpretation and identifying the original author's intended meaning. Bock and Blaising advocate a historical-grammatical-literary-theological method of interpretation. They claim that this has much in common with the historical-grammatical method of interpretation, but this method is a significant departure from the teachings of Ryrie and Chafer. While there are some differences in the way that Chafer and Ryrie employed typology, they do not seem significant enough to argue that classical dispensationalists and essentialist dispensationalists do not really employ a literal method of interpretation. While Chafer certainly made mistakes in some of his identifications of typology, it is not fair to say that he did not interpret the Bible literally.

Dispensationalism," *Journal of Ministry and Theology* 1, no. 1 (Spring 1997): 6–37.

4
Chafer's Theological System: Soteriology

This and following chapters address several aspects of Chafer's theological system. They are by no means exhaustive; instead, they focus on some of the unique aspects of Chafer's system as well as some of his beliefs that are directly related to his dispensational system. As a result, his soteriology and sanctification are discussed because of his unique contributions among dispensational authors. Chafer's view of the relationship between the church and Israel, his view of the dispensations and the covenants, as well as his eschatology are also addressed.

SOTERIOLOGY

Chafer's Soteriology

One of the most significant contributions Chafer made to systematic theology is his emphasis on salvation by grace through faith alone. In many ways, Chafer made significant progress in recovering the free grace position of soteriology. This chapter gives a brief description of Chafer's soteriology. Like the other sections it is not exhaustive but simply emphasizes unique contributions that Chafer made in this area.

Chafer's Definition of Soteriology

Chafer defines soteriology as "that portion of Systematic Theology which treats of salvation."[1] His discussion on salvation in his *Systematic Theology* is much broader than solely focusing on individual salvation as most theologians do when discussing soteriology. Chafer's volume on soteriology contains the following major topics: the person of the Savior, divine election, the saving work of the Triune God, the eternal security of the believer, as well as the terms of salvation.

Chafer's Discussion of Soteriology

The first section focuses on the person of the Savior. He distinguishes his purpose in this section from his volume on Christology as follows:

> Volume V in this work on Systematic Theology is assigned to the pursuance of Christology. On those pages a more orderly and comprehensive treatment of that great theme will be undertaken. As stated above, under trinitarianism, specific consideration has been given to Christ's Person. Under Soteriology (apart from an introductory word), specific consideration is to be given to Christ's work, while under Christology these two fundamental truths are to be considered together. As before intimated, it is essential, when approaching the study of the work of Christ, to restate or review

---

[1] Lewis Sperry Chafer, *Systematic Theology*, vol. 3, *Soteriology* (Grand Rapids, MI: Kregel Publications, 1993), 3.

certain facts relative to His Person to the end that some larger recognition may be secured about who it is that undertakes to provide so great a salvation. Attention is therefore first directed to the Person of the Savior.[2]

In this section, Chafer primarily focuses on how the person of Christ made Him eligible to perform the work of salvation. Thus, Chafer begins by discussing Christ's person. Chafer focuses on Christ's seven positions (for example, the preincarnate Christ, the incarnate Christ, Christ in His death, the resurrected Christ, Christ ascended and seated in heaven, Christ returning, and Christ reigning forever), His offices (for example, prophet, priest, and king), His sonship (the Son of God, the Son of Man, the Son of David and the Son of Abraham), as well as the hypostatic union.

Chafer then discusses Christ's work. He begins by describing Christ's sufferings in life and death. Chafer addresses the results of Christ's suffering in life and death (i.e. a substitution for sinners, the ending of the law principle on behalf of those who are saved, redemption toward sin, reconciliation toward Man, propitiation toward God, the judgment of the sin nature, the ground of the believer's forgiveness and cleansing, the ground for the deferring of righteous divine judgments, the taking away of pre-cross sin once covered by sacrifice, the national salvation of Israel, the millennial and eternal blessings upon Gentiles, the spoiling of principalities and powers, the ground of peace, and the purification of things in heaven).

---

[2] Ibid., 11.

With respect to the national salvation of Israel, Chafer by no means implies that all Jews will be saved apart from salvation in Christ. Instead, Chafer argues that the salvation promised by the Old Testament prophets would be made possible by the death of Christ (cf. Jeremiah 31:33–34, Romans 11:27, Isaiah 53, et al.). He writes:

> It has been observed that, in the age that is past, Jehovah's dealing with Israel's sins—even the sins for which appointed sacrifices were presented—was only a temporary covering of those sins, and that Christ in His death bore the judgment of those sins which Jehovah had before passed over; but the final application of the value of Christ's death in behalf of Israel awaits the moment of her national conversion (cf. Isaiah 66:8, a nation born "at once"—*pa_.am*—literally, as a time measurement, "a stroke," or "the beat of a foot"). It is then that, according to His covenant, Jehovah will "take away" their sins.[3]

Thus, Chafer argues that the national conversion will be the time of the national salvation of Israel. He does not in any way imply that Israelites will be saved by their physical descendancy alone, apart from faith.

Chafer then has a chapter on the types of Christ's suffering and death. His view on typology was already discussed in the chapter on methodology, so it is not addressed in detail here. However, types of Christ's death in Chafer's *Systematic Theology* include everything from the two birds in

---

[3] Ibid., 106.

Leviticus 14:1–7, to the Old Testament sacrifices, to the tabernacle.

In chapter six of his volume on soteriology in his *Systematic Theology*, Chafer defines the following important terms: atonement, expiation, forgiveness and remission, guilt, justice, justification, penalty, propitiation, reconciliation, redemption and ransom, sacrifice, satisfaction, vicarious, and substitutionary. This step is important for traditional dispensationalism. Key terms need to be defined. The postmodern tendency is to utilize the same terms in multiple ways to communicate similarity when there truly are significant distinctions. However, by clearly defining terms such as these, one is forced to identify similarities and differences.

In chapter seven, Chafer discusses true and false theories regarding the value of Christ's death. He covers theories of the atonement as well as a historical discussion on the topic. Once again, Chafer discusses typology related to the value of Christ's death, "Since so much typology pertains to the death of Christ, this peculiar body of truth must be given its full import if the full value of Christ's death is to be recognized. That it is omitted from practically all theological discussions regarding Christ's death is a self-evident fact and the effect of its neglect is obvious."[4]

Chafer also discusses divine election. He covers some of the key terms related to election and then addresses some essential truths regarding election. Chafer affirms that by election God has chosen some to salvation but not all. According to Chafer, divine election was accomplished in

---

[4] Ibid., 135.

eternity past. He believes that election does not rest merely on foreknowledge. He affirms the immutability of election as well as briefly addresses the issue of the order of God's divine decrees.[5] He also addresses some of the key objections to election.

Chafer also addresses the issue of the extent of the atonement. Chafer discusses the different views of the atonement and ultimately supports an unlimited view of the atonement. He does so based on a literal interpretation of the Bible: "This form of moderate Calvinism is more the belief of Bible expositors than of the theologians, which fact is doubtless due to the truth that the Bible, taken in its natural terminology and apart from those strained interpretations which are required to defend a theory, seems to teach an unlimited redemption."[6] He also argues this position based on the separation between the church and Israel. Finally, he raises the question of whether the gospel can be universally preached on a personal basis under a limited atonement perspective. Thus, Chafer develops his argument on the extent of the atonement from a Biblical, theological, and logical perspective.

Chafer also discusses the finished work of Christ. In this section, he concludes the following:

> Attention has been called before to the truth that what is termed *the finished work of Christ* [emphasis his] includes a threefold contemplation of the value of Christ's death as related to the unsaved. That death is a redemption toward sin, a reconciliation toward man, and

---

[5] This section summarizes the headings found in Ibid., 172–75.
[6] Ibid., 184.

> a propitiation toward God. No one, or even two, of these aspects of Christ's death for the unsaved will represent a full exhibition of that specific phase of His death. All three are required; but the three together form a perfect whole which is properly termed *the finished work of Christ* [emphasis his]. No aspect of the sin problem can be conceived which does not find its solution in this threefold achievement.[7]

Once again, he clearly addresses the terms in order to avoid confusion. As a result of his view of the finished work of Christ, Chafer considers faith alone to be necessary for salvation:

> These effective factors in Christ's death for the unsaved are not even remotely within the range of human cooperation. In relation to this threefold work of Christ, man can sustain no part in it other than to *believe* [emphasis his] that it avails for him. To those who believe, the whole value of Christ's finished work is reckoned and, because of that reckoning, they stand at once redeemed from condemnation because of sin, reconciled with respect to their own relation to God, and sheltered perfectly under that satisfaction which Christ offered to outraged holiness. By so much, the one who believes is forevermore upon a peace footing with God (Rom. 5:1).[8]

Since the work of the cross is completed, the only proper response is to believe, according to Chafer.

---

[7] Ibid., 208.
[8] Ibid.

Chafer also discusses eternal security. He defines eternal security as, "those chosen of God and saved by grace are, of necessity, preserved unto the realization of the design of God."[9] Whereas some Calvinists argue that perseverance of the saints implies that a true believer will never fall away, Chafer defines the term of eternal security in terms of the preservation of the believer according to God's design when he writes:

> In general, the New Testament presents the Father as purposing, calling, justifying, and glorifying those who believe on Christ; the Son is presented as becoming incarnate that He might be a Kinsman-Redeemer, as dying a substitutionary and efficacious death, as rising to be a living Savior both as Advocate and Intercessor, and as Head over all things to the Church; the Holy Spirit is presented as administering and executing the purpose of the Father and the redemption which the Son has wrought. It is reasonable, then, that all three Persons of the Godhead should have their individual share in preserving to fruition that which God has determined.[10]

Thus, Chafer defines eternal security in terms of what God does to preserve the believer as opposed to what the believer must do.

This relates to Chafer's next discussion of the terms of salvation. First, he discusses the concept of repent and believe. He argues that the concept of repentance involves a change of

---

[9] Ibid., 268.
[10] Ibid., 315.

mind. He describes the relationship of repentance to saving faith as follows:

> Too often, when it is asserted—as it is here—that repentance is not to be added to belief as a separate requirement for salvation, it is assumed that by so much the claim has been set up that repentance is *not* necessary to salvation. Therefore, it is as dogmatically stated as language can declare, that repentance is essential to salvation and that none could be saved apart from repentance, but it is included in believing and could not be separated from it.[11]

Chafer believes that repentance is included in the process of believing. According to Chafer, salvation is "not turning from something to something; but rather turning to something from something."[12] To a certain degree, Chafer believes that repentance is not from sin for salvation but is synonymous with saving faith which is a change of mind about God.

Chafer also argues that public confession of belief in the gospel is not required for salvation. He writes, "Confession of Christ is a Christian's privilege and duty and may be undertaken at the moment one is saved, but it is not a condition of salvation by grace, else works of merit intrude where only the work of God reigns."[13] Chafer's view of the gospel is intimately connected with his perspective on evangelism. For instance, he says:

---

[11] Ibid., 373.
[12] Ibid., 374.
[13] Ibid., 380.

> Special care must be exercised by preachers who are called upon to preach the gospel to groups and congregations. The gospel must be presented in its purity and no requirement laid upon the unsaved respecting works they might perform. Public methods often imply that there is saving value in something the unsaved are asked to do. God not only calls out His elect people through gospel preaching, but He ever cares for those whom He saves. If evangelizing methods do not contradict these great truths, there will be less unhappy results.[14]

As this quote indicates, Chafer is very concerned about using excessive means that tend to relate works to simple faith in Christ. This is likely a result of his past experience traveling with evangelists like Reverend A. T. Reed. It is also a reflection of Chafer's Calvinistic tendencies:

> Language cannot be more explicit; and in truth were it not for the enlightening work of the Spirit by which He convicts of sin, of righteousness, and of judgment (John 16:7–11), no unregenerate person would ever turn to Christ for salvation. The point at issue is that, when the Spirit undertakes His work of bringing men to Christ, there will be little need of persuasive methods. The Holy Spirit uses the Word of God on the lips of a devoted servant of God or on a printed page, and men hearing the truth and believing are saved. From that time forth,

---

[14] Lewis Sperry Chafer, *Systematic Theology*, vol. 7, *Doctrinal Summarization* (Grand Rapids, MI: Kregel Publications, 1993), 144.

all who are saved occupy the Christian's position and have a definite responsibility to witness, not to the end they may thereby be saved but because they are saved.[15]

Chafer truly believes that salvation is a work of the Holy Spirit, and it is through the power of God and not necessarily through the influence of man.

As a result of Chafer's view of evangelism, he emphasizes the importance of sharing the gospel of saving grace alone:

> Outside The Doctrines related to the Person and work of Christ, there is no truth more far-reaching in its implications and no fact more to be defended than that salvation in all its limitless magnitude is secured, so far as human responsibility is concerned, by believing on Christ as Savior. To this one requirement no other obligation may be added without violence to the Scriptures and total disruption of the essential doctrine of salvation by grace alone. Only ignorance or reprehensible inattention to the structure of a right Soteriology will attempt to intrude some form of human works with its supposed merit into that which, if done at all, must, by the very nature of the case, be wrought by God alone and on the principle of sovereign grace. But few, indeed, seem ever to comprehend the doctrine of sovereign grace, and it is charitable, at least, to revert to this fact as the explanation of the all-but-universal disposition to confuse the vital issues involved. It is the

---

[15] Ibid., 145.

> purpose of this section to demonstrate that the eternal glories which are wrought in sovereign grace are conditioned, on the human side, by faith alone. The practical bearing of this truth must of necessity make drastic claims upon the preacher and become a qualifying influence in the soul-winning methods which are employed. The student would do well to bring his message and his methods into complete agreement with the workings of divine grace, rather than to attempt to conform this unalterable truth to human ideals.[16]

Chafer's view can be summarized as "salvation by grace alone through faith alone in Christ alone." Chafer's view of the gospel is discussed in his book *Salvation*. He wrote the book in order to present a "simple Gospel message." It was not ultimately "intended to be a contribution to a theological discussion" because it was "evangelistic in purpose."[17] In this book he wrote a chapter on "The One Condition of Salvation" and he says:

> The one word *believe* represents all a sinner can do and all a sinner must do to be saved. It is believing the record God has given of His Son. In this record it is stated that He has entered into all the needs of our lost condition and is alive from the dead to be a living Savior to all who put their trust in Him. It is quite possible for any intelligent person to know whether he has placed

---

[16] Ibid., vol. 3, 371.
[17] Lewis Sperry Chafer, *Salvation* (Grand Rapids, MI: Kregel Publications, 1991), 9.

such confidence in the Savior. Saving faith is a matter of personal consciousness.[18]

The chapters in *Salvation* describe some of Chafer's major beliefs. Ultimately Chafer's soteriology emphasized the lostness of humanity, the one condition of belief for salvation, assurance of salvation, eternal rewards, and the eternal security of the believer.

Thus, in Chafer's *Systematic Theology*, he denies the saving nature of baptismal regeneration, surrender to God, and confession of sin, as well as imploring God to save. With respect to his denial of the necessity of surrender to God as part of the salvation process, Chafer writes:

> On account of its subtlety due to its pious character, no confusing intrusion into the doctrine that salvation is conditioned alone upon believing is more effective than the added demand that the unsaved must dedicate themselves to do God's will in their daily life, as well as to believe upon Christ. The desirability of a dedication to God on the part of every believer is obvious and is so stressed in the Sacred Text that many sincere people who are inattentive to doctrine are easily led to suppose that this same dedication, which is *voluntary* in the case of the believer, is *imperative* in the case of the unsaved. This aspect of this general theme may be approached under three considerations of it: (1) the incapacity of the

---

[18] Ibid., 47.

unsaved, (2) what is involved, and (3) the preacher's responsibility.[19]

As this statement suggests, Chafer questions how the unsaved could possibly respond to the demand of some preachers to surrender his life when it is impossible for him to do so. Chafer argues that this confuses salvation with sanctification:

> The error of imposing Christ's Lordship upon the unsaved is disastrous even though they are not able intelligently to resent it or to remind the preacher of the fact that he, in calling upon them to dedicate their lives, is demanding of them what they have no ability to produce. A destructive heresy is abroad under the name The Oxford Movement, which specializes in this blasting error, except that the promoters of the Movement omit altogether the idea of believing on Christ for salvation and promote exclusively the obligation to surrender to God. They substitute consecration for conversion, faithfulness for faith, and beauty of daily life for believing unto eternal life.[20]

Some, like John MacArthur, have criticized Chafer for this emphasis,[21] but most proponents of the free grace position of

---

[19] Chafer, *Systematic Theology*, vol. 3, 384–85.
[20] Ibid., 385.
[21] See John MacArthur, *The Gospel According to Jesus: What Does Jesus Mean When He Says "Follow Me?"*, rev. and expanded ed. (Grand Rapids, MI: Zondervan Publishing House, 1994), 30. On page 30 of this book, MacArthur accuses Chafer of coming up with an entirely new way of looking at the gospel which no "serious theologian" would have entertained before this century.

salvation consider Chafer to be a key person for rediscovering the essence of the gospel of grace.[22]

One argument that should be addressed is whether Chafer taught two ways of salvation as some allege. He makes a statement about this issue when he writes:

> Are there, then, two ways to be saved today? The dispensationalist says No, because he recognizes Judaism to be in abeyance at the present time, and this text of Luke 10, which might be called the *John 3:16 of Judaism* [emphasis his], does not apply to believers today. But the Covenant theologian, who must include well-nigh everything in his system of teaching, is faced with both statements on the lips of Christ.[23]

This statement in and of itself is a little confusing. On the one hand, he clearly states that there are not two ways of salvation. However, one could argue that he is saying in this statement that there is one way today (salvation by grace through faith) but in the previous time there was obedience to the law. However, this potential problem might be clarified by another of Chafer's statement, "Nor is the situation relieved for those who claim that the Law has ceased as a means of justification; for it was never that, nor could it be (Galatians 3:11)."[24] These

---

[22] Some have rightly argued that the grace of God was Chafer's central interpretive motif. For more information see Bruce A. Baker, "The Theological Method of Lewis Sperry Chafer," *Journal of Ministry and Theology* 5 (Spring 2001): 65–67.

[23] Lewis Sperry Chafer, "Are There Two Ways to Be Saved?" *Bibliotheca Sacra* 105, no. 417 (January–March 1948): 2.

[24] Lewis Sperry Chafer, "Dispensationalism," *Bibliotheca Sacra* 93, no. 372 (October –December 1936): 415.

statements should definitively clear up any argument to the contrary.

Chafer's Soteriology Compared with Ryrie's

While Ryrie does not represent all essentialist dispensationalists, he likely represents the majority of them. Essentialist dispensationalists typically embrace a free grace view of the Gospel. Like Chafer, this is likely due to an emphasis on the literal interpretation of the Bible in light of dispensational considerations. This section emphasizes the continuity between Ryrie's and Chafer's soteriology.[25]

Ryrie's approach to soteriology is very similar to Chafer's. For instance, his overall categories in *Basic Theology* are very similar to Chafer's: Biblical terminology, the passion of Christ, the meaning of the death of Christ, some results of salvation, theories of the atonement, the doctrine of election, the extent of the atonement, the application of salvation, the security of the believer, and the essence of the gospel.[26] Like Chafer, Ryrie espouses unlimited atonement as well as a moderate form of Calvinism. Like Chafer, Ryrie is very concerned about fallacies that accompany the proclamation of the gospel. He rejects baptismal regeneration. Ryrie defines repentance as "a change of mind about someone or something

---

[25] This approach is by no means exhaustive. For a more exhaustive discussion of Ryrie's soteriology please consult Charles Caldwell Ryrie, *So Great Salvation: What It Means to Believe in Jesus Christ* (Wheaton, IL: Victor Books, 1989).

[26] Ryrie, Charles Caldwell Ryrie, *Basic Theology: A Popular Systemic Guide to Understanding Biblical Truth* (Chicago, IL: Moody Press, 1999), 7.

in a way that effects some change in the individual."[27] He defines saving repentance in this way: "This saving repentance has to involve a change of mind about Jesus Christ so that whatever a person thought of Him before, he changes his mind and trusts Him to be his Savior."[28] Ryrie defines Lordship Salvation as "that teaching that to be saved a person must not only trust Jesus as Savior but also Lord of his life, submitting (or at least being willing to submit) his life to His sovereign authority."[29] Ryrie rejects this teaching and believes that repentance is a change of mind about God. Like Chafer, he believes that it is part of the process of belief. He also rejects the concepts of total surrender and repentance from sin as being essential to the gospel.

Chafer's Soteriology Compared with Bock's

Since progressive dispensationalists tend to have a much more diverse approach to many aspects of theology, one cannot generalize about how all progressive or traditional dispensationalists view soteriology. Since there is not a systematic theology written from a progressive dispensationalist perspective, one cannot make a summary of a comprehensive view of soteriology from a progressive dispensational perspective. This section reviews an article written by Darrell L. Bock in order to make some observations of his soteriological view. While one cannot make a definitive conclusion on how his progressive dispensational view affects

---

[27] Ryrie, *So Great Salvation: What It Means to Believe in Jesus Christ*, 157.
[28] Ryrie, *Basic Theology*, 390.
[29] Ryrie, *So Great Salvation: What It Means to Believe in Jesus Christ*, 156.

his soteriological conclusions, one can note his methodological attempt to find a mediating position between both camps.

First, it should be noted that salvation is not discussed substantially in *Progressive Dispensationalism*. Only a passing reference is made in order to justify an already-not-yet hermeneutic. Bock and Blaising make a comparison between the fact that believers are already saved, but God is going to complete the salvation process in the future. As a result, they conclude, "In one sense, salvation has arrived; in another I await it. In the cases of both salvation and the kingdom of God, one should pay attention to which side of the relationship is highlighted in any given text."[30] From this statement, one may conclude that Bock and Blaising believe in eternal security (else one could not really say they are saved at this point unless they are noting that they could potentially lose it), but little else can be ascertained.

A more detailed but not comprehensive example of Bock's soteriology is found in his review of John MacArthur's *The Gospel According to Jesus*.[31] His evaluation of MacArthur's work shows some distinction to Ryrie and Chafer.[32] He defines

---

[30] Craig A. Blaising and Darrell L. Bock, *Progressive Dispensationalism* (Wheaton, IL: BridgePoint, 1993), 98.

[31] Darrell L. Bock, "A Review of the Gospel According to Jesus," *Bibliotheca Sacra* 146, no. 581 (January–March 1989): 21–40.

[32] It should be noted that there are differing opinions regarding Lordship Salvation among those who hold to progressive and traditional dispensationalistm. There are progressive and traditional dispensationalists on each side of the debate. This comparison does not in any way imply that Bock is less of a dispensationalist because he does not hold a free grace position on salvation. Instead, it is simply emphasizing discontinuity with Bock when compared to Chafer and Ryrie. The key point of emphasis is that the same methodology that tries to find a mediating position between two opposing camps may be more

repentance as "a change of view with reference to sin, self, and Jesus."[33] He acknowledges, however, that "the working out of the details of repentance is not as complex a process as some of MacArthur's language suggests."[34] Like Ryrie, Bock believes one can repent about several things. However, he seems to apply this idea of repentance without making a distinction between general repentance and saving repentance when he writes:

> In the Lucan expression of the Great Commission, Jesus told the disciples to preach repentance to all the nations starting from Jerusalem (Luke 24:47). This shows that repentance is an appropriate term to use when speaking of the gospel. The reference to Gentiles in that verse indicates that the gospel applies not merely to Jews but universally to all. Faith is usually stressed because it is the positive term and is the flip side of repentance. When a person places his faith in Christ, he is at that moment repenting. The two go together, hand in glove. In salvation, an individual changes his mind about sin and about his inability to overcome it on his own, and he turns to Jesus and trusts Him to deal with his need. Luke 5:31–32 illustrates that in repenting, a person is acknowledging he has a need, because he is spiritually sick and comes to the Great Physician humbly for spiritual healing.[35]

---

common among progressive dispensationalists who occasionally try to do the same in other areas of theology.
[33] Ibid., 28.
[34] Ibid.
[35] Ibid.

In this statement Bock seems to confuse several things. First, he seems to both be arguing for repentance as a change of mind about Christ as well as a change of mind about sin at the same time. Bock selectively cites Chafer in defense of his position, but he uses the concept of repentance in a way that is foreign to what Chafer thought:

> What Chafer argued is that repentance alone, without the positive side of faith, is not enough. Regret or sorrow for sin is not enough if it is not wedded to trust. When Chafer affirmed that repentance alone is inadequate for salvation, he had in mind the idea of sorrow associated with the "anxiety benches" in the tent revivals of his day. Chafer's remarks need to be understood in their historical context.[36]

In Bock's defense, he likely is disputing a view of repentance as advocated by Zane Hodges as described in *Absolutely Free!* more than the views expressed by Chafer or Ryrie. While the historical context is important, one must note that Bock ascribes a use of the term repentance to Chafer in a way that is inconsistent with how he used it. Chafer never defines saving repentance as "regret or sorrow for sin" and requires that to be wedded to trust. Instead, he argues for the change of mind about God to occur simultaneously with trust. This shows a major methodological distinction between Bock and Chafer. While Chafer clearly defines his terms with plenty of Scriptural references and states his theology in light of those

---

[36] Ibid., 28–29.

terms, Bock utilizes the same term without clear definition in inconsistent ways. As a result, he finds more continuity with Chafer's view than Chafer himself would have claimed. These types of methodological distinctions are not limited to soteriology.

Unlike Ryrie and Chafer, Bock speaks of a saving confession when he writes, "The frequent statements in the Scriptures that speak of Jesus being confessed in salvation as 'the Lord Jesus' make it inadvisable to limit the saving confession to just the title Savior. MacArthur cites Acts 2:21, 36; 16:31; and Romans 10:9–10 as examples."[37] Once again, neither Ryrie nor Chafer connect confession to salvation, nor do they see the confession of Lordship as essential to that process. Bock also seems to see perseverance of the saints in terms of the believer's continuing commitment to God, "A total turning away is evidence of the absence of saving faith. Where there is total denial, there is no faith and thus no assurance."[38] Bock defines these practical tests of saving faith: (1) total callousness toward sin (this indicates that one is not truly saved), (2) no evidence of fruit, and (3) a desire of intimacy with God the Father.[39] Ryrie argues that there are subjective and objective tests of assurance. The objective test is that God's Word declares that one is saved through faith. The subjective relates to experiences. Subjective experiences include obedience of commands, loving other believers, and doing right.[40] Chafer also lists both objective and subjective tests of saving faith: the

---

[37] Ibid., 29.
[38] Ibid., 30.
[39] Ibid., 30.
[40] Ryrie, *So Great Salvation: What It Means to Believe in Jesus Christ*, 143.

knowledge of God as Father, a new reality in prayer, a new ability to understand the Scriptures, a new sense of the sinfulness of sin, a new love for the unsaved, a new love for the saved, a manifestation of the character of Christ, and a consciousness of salvation through faith in Christ.[41] They also seem to agree with Ryrie that the subjective should not be the primary determiner of saving faith when they write: "It should be recognized that a carnal Christian is as perfectly saved as the spiritual Christian; for no experience, or merit, or service can form any part of the grounds of salvation."[42]

Additionally, Bock defines the necessity of the Lordship of Christ for salvation differently than both MacArthur and Chafer. He writes:

> In confessing Jesus as Lord (Romans 10:9), and coming to Him in faith for salvation, a person is acknowledging that Jesus has authority at three levels: the authority to save, the authority to be honored, and the authority to be followed. A person coming to Christ may not consciously be acknowledging all three levels at the moment of salvation, but in turning to the Lord in dependence on Him, all three are present.[43]

He further alludes to the doctrinal statement of Dallas Theological Seminary for support of his position:

---

[41] Lewis Sperry Chafer, *Major Bible Themes: 52 Vital Doctrines of the Scriptures Simplified and Explained*, rev. John F. Walvoord, rev. ed. (Grand Rapids, MI: Zondervan Publishing House, 1974) 214–16.
[42] Ibid., 214.
[43] Bock, "A Review of the Gospel According to Jesus," 33.

> Article XXI of Dallas Seminary's Doctrinal Statement reads, "We believe that at death the spirits and souls of those who have trusted in the *Lord* Jesus Christ for salvation pass immediately into His presence" (italics added). The point of citing the Doctrinal Statement is not to argue that it settles the issue, but to show that within the tradition of the Seminary many elements of belief that MacArthur denies to the school's tradition and to some of its former faculty members are in fact present in it, at least to some degree. That Jesus is confessed as Lord is one of those elements.[44]

Bock's statement argues that the Dallas Theological Seminary doctrinal statement includes a view of Lordship that is at least similar to his. However, Chafer, who authored the doctrinal statement, does not appear to have the same definition of Lord as Bock:

> It cannot be unobserved that the confession of verses 9 and 10 [Romans 10:9–10] is declared to be a calling on the name of the Lord. In other words, this confession is that unavoidable acknowledgment to God on the part of the one who is exercising saving faith, that he accepts Christ as his Savior. As Abraham *amened* [emphasis his] the promise of God—not a mere unresponsive believing (Genesis 15:6; Romans 4:3), so the trusting soul responds to the promise which God proffers of salvation through Christ.[45]

---

[44] Ibid., 30. Italics are added by Bock.
[45] Chafer, *Systematic Theology*, vol. 3, 380.

Chafer does not seem to define Christ's Lordship in terms of authority to rule but in His faithfulness as God to fulfill His promises. Once again, Bock uses the same terms as traditional dispensationalists, but he defines them differently. As a result, one cannot identify continuity between the soteriology of both groups but discontinuity.

Ultimately, Bock attempts to come to a mediating position between Chafer and MacArthur. He writes:

> In the current debate about the gospel each side is expressing legitimate concerns, concerns that are biblical and that need attention. Chafer and Hodges are rightly concerned about grace and assurance, for these are key themes of the New Testament. MacArthur is right in raising the question of false profession. But the danger is that in defending their passionate concerns, they may each be giving up the opposite concern that also needs integration into the picture.[46]

As a result, he tries to identify a mediating position that balances both views. This preferred method of finding a compromise between two competing views is not limited to soteriology. To a certain degree, progressive dispensationalism has been embraced by some as a mediating position between Covenant Theology and dispensationalism. In the end, Bock concludes:

> This alternative view focuses on the relational element of saving faith, which is directed not merely at

---

[46] Bock, "A Review of the Gospel According to Jesus," 37.

propositions but to a Person. One believes and trusts in a Person and His work. The Person is the Lord Jesus and the work is what He accomplished on the cross. This dependence recognizes Jesus' authority to save, to be honored, and to be followed. It does not 'quantify' the gospel; rather it rests on the quality of the Person who saves and on the recognition of the quality and nature of that One to accomplish what He promises.[47]

Thus, Bock believes that saving faith involves acknowledging God's authority to rule over one's life but not necessarily the authority over every area of life.

Summary of Soteriological Observations

Chafer's *Systematic Theology* deals with the topic of soteriology in great detail. Chafer's soteriology reflects a moderate Calvinist position which emphasizes the role of faith alone in salvation. He defines repentance as a change of mind about Christ which ultimately is part of saving faith. He affirms the security of the believer by emphasizing God's role in ensuring the believer's eternal destiny. The analysis of Ryrie's position on these issues reflects continuity with Chafer.

While his treatment in his *Basic Theology* is not quite as extensive as Chafer's (probably due to the comparative size of both works), they agree on most points. The analysis of Bock's view has some similarities but also dissimilarities with Ryrie and Chafer. Methodologically, he tries to emphasize continuity with Chafer by using the same terms he does, but his use reflects a different definition. He attempts to find a mediating

---

[47] Bock, "A Review of the Gospel According to Jesus," 38–39.

position between what he considers to be the two extremes of Hodges and MacArthur (and in some instances Chafer). This methodological goal is likely reflected in other aspects of Bock's theological method.

5

Chafer's Theological System: Sanctification

Another significant aspect of Chafer's theological method is his emphasis on sanctification. His book *He That is Spiritual* is one of his greatest contributions in this area. This section analyzes the unique aspects of Chafer's view of sanctification.

SANCTIFICATION

Sanctification in Chafer's *Systematic Theology*

Chafer discusses several aspects of sanctification in his *Systematic Theology*.[1] He begins by defining the key terms associated with sanctification (i.e. sanctify, holy, and saint). He also addresses the means by which God sanctifies the believer. Included in this discussion is how a believer can set himself apart to God. Chafer addresses the three aspects of sanctification: positional, experimental, and ultimate sanctification. According to Chafer, the three agents of sanctification are the Son, the Spirit, and the truth of God.

---

[1] This section is a summary of Chafer, *Systematic Theology*, vol. 7, 274–84.

Chafer's View of Sanctification in *He That Is Spiritual*

Chafer's main argument in *He That is Spiritual* is that "true spirituality is that quality of life in the child of God which satisfies and glorifies the Father."[2] He recognizes the potential areas for disagreement, but he tries to emphasize areas of consensus:

> The Bible doctrine concerning the Christian's nature and daily practice, and the relation of these to the death of Christ, is subject to some disagreement. It is not the primary purpose of this book to correct details of doctrine. The object has been rather to state the outstanding revelation of the divine provision for the overcoming life. May we be delivered from controversy over secondary things in the face of our present failure to "walk as it becometh saints."[3]

Chafer's view of sanctification that was expressed in this book deals with the role of God in securing sanctification as well as the role that the individual Christian played in relying on the Holy Spirit. Chafer equates relying on the Holy Spirit to "walking by means of the Holy Spirit."[4]

He That is Spiritual outlines several aspects of Chafer's view of sanctification. Chafer begins by a discussion on the three classes of men: the natural man, the carnal man, and the

---

[2] Lewis Sperry Chafer, *He That Is Spiritual: A Classic Study of the Biblical Doctrine of Spirituality*, Rev. ed. (Grand Rapids, MI: Zondervan Publishing House, 1967), 7.
[3] Ibid.
[4] Ibid., 132.

spiritual man. According to Chafer the natural man is unregenerate and unchanged spiritually; the carnal man is a babe in Christ who walks like a man; the spiritual man is able to understand "the divine ideal in life and ministry, in power with God and man, in unbroken fellowship and blessing."[5] The intent of Chafer's book is to encourage people to live the life of the spiritual man.

According to Chafer, one of the keys for being a spiritual man is the filling of the Spirit. He writes:

> Spirituality is not gained in answer to prevailing prayer; for there is little Scripture to warrant the believer to be praying for the filling of the Spirit. It is the *normal* work of the Spirit to fill the one who is rightly adjusted to God. The Christian will always be filled while he is making the work of the Spirit possible in his life.[6]

Rather than praying or waiting for the filling of the Spirit, Chafer advised believers to "grieve not the Holy Spirit" and "quench not the Holy Spirit." Chafer defines grieving the Holy Spirit as "retaining unconfessed any known sin."[7] Additionally, he must not quench the Holy Spirit by showing any "unyieldedness to the revealed will of God."[8] In a positive sense, the believer must walk by means of the Holy Spirit. As previously mentioned, this involves relying on the Holy Spirit.[9] According to Chafer, this is "imperative because of the

---

[5] Ibid., 22.
[6] Ibid., 67.
[7] Ibid., 96.
[8] Ibid., 86.
[9] Ibid., 132.

impossible heavenly calling, the opposing power of Satan, and the continued presence of the 'flesh' with its Adamic nature."[10] Thus, Chafer considered the Adamic nature to still be present in the spiritual man, but he is commanded to have victory over it.

Chafer has been accused by some as being overly influenced by the Keswick movement as well as the notion of the second blessing. Warfield accuses him of making "use of all the jargon of the Higher Life teachers" but also recognizes that "there are lengths, nevertheless, to which Mr. Chafer will not go with his Higher Life friends."[11] Warfield and other critics do at least acknowledge that Chafer would not teach the possibility of sinless perfection on this side of heaven. Chafer writes, "There is complete deliverance by the Spirit for every child of God, but this should not be confused with any use of the word 'perfect' when the incapacity to sin is implied by the use of that word."[12] Instead, he emphasizes the three-fold view of sanctification. Chafer defines sanctification as being "set apart or classified; usually as pertaining to God."[13] Therefore, Chafer describes positional sanctification, experimental sanctification, and ultimate sanctification. According to Chafer, "all believers are positionally sanctified in Christ 'once and for all' at the moment they are saved. This sanctification is as perfect as He is perfect."[14] Experimental sanctification is the progressive process of the believer becoming yielded to God,

---

[10] Ibid.
[11] Benjamin B. Warfield, "A Review of Lewis Sperry Chafer's 'He That Is Spiritual'," *The Princeton Theological Review* Vol. XVII, no. 2 (April 1919): 322.
[12] Chafer, *He That Is Spiritual*, 106.
[13] Ibid., 107.
[14] Ibid., 108.

being delivered from sin, and growing in Christ. This all occurs by the power of God through the Spirit and through the Word of God according to Chafer.[15] According to Chafer, ultimate sanctification is when all believers are "perfected in glory into the very image of the Son of God."[16] In Chafer's opinion, one cannot reach this point in this earthly life. He writes, "The Bible, therefore, does not teach that any child of God is wholly sanctified in daily life before that final consummation of all things." Thus, Chafer distinguishes between a progressive experimental sanctification and a future ultimate sanctification in which sin is no longer possible for the believer. Unlike some Keswick teachers, he does not imply that all willful sin can be eradicated in this life.

Chafer also clearly disagrees with those within the Keswick movement who argued for a second work of grace:

> The failure to discern that the Holy Spirit indwells every believer was the common and all but universal error of men two generations ago. That error was promoted in the early Keswick conferences and received and taught generally throughout Great Britain and America. However, American expositors of the last two generations have done much to recover this important doctrine from this and other similar misconceptions. The notion that the Holy Spirit is received as a second work of grace is now defended only by extreme holiness groups. In other words, it is more clearly understood than it was earlier that there can be no such a thing as a

---

[15] Ibid., 107–08.
[16] Ibid., 109.

> Christian who is not indwelt by the Holy Spirit. This truth is so emphatically declared in the New Testament that it seems almost impossible that any other view could ever have been entertained. It will be remembered that the ministry of the Spirit as One who indwells is but one of His present benefits and is not to be confused with His baptism, His sealing, or His filling. Of these other works, more will yet be presented. Though, as has been observed, the presence of the Holy Spirit in the believer may not be indicated by any corresponding revolutionary experience, His indwelling is nonetheless one of the most characterizing of all the features which constitute a Christian what he is (cf. Romans 8:8–9).[17]

In this quote Chafer separates himself from the Keswicks because he could not advocate some of the views that were espoused in the early Keswick conferences.[18]

However, Chafer did appreciate the emphasis the Keswick movement brought to Bible conferences regarding the work of the Holy Spirit:

> Bible teachers and expositors generally have sought to overcome the effects of the neglect of the doctrine of the Holy Spirit in usual theological disciplines by special emphasis upon these themes. The church of the present generation owes much to the Keswick movement of

---

[17] Lewis Sperry Chafer, *Systematic Theology*, vol. 6, *Pneumatology* (Grand Rapids, MI: Kregel Publications, 1993), 122.
[18] Cf. J. Robertson McQuilkin, "The Keswick Perspective," in *Five Views of Sanctification*, ed. Stanley N. Gundry (Grand Rapids, MI: Zondervan Publishing House, 1987) 151–183. McQuilkin provides a historical overview that discusses many central Keswick beliefs.

England and its extensive testimony in this and other lands. The inclusion of these subjects in modern Bible study conventions and by men able to speak with authority has done much to give these doctrines their rightful emphasis. A great theologian who has written massive treatises on the Person and work of Christ but who practically never ventures into the field of the Person and work of the Holy Spirit may be credited with such testimony as he has given, but must, at the same time, suffer discredit for the encouragement he has given to neglect of such vital truth on the part of all who follow him. That this presentation of Systematic Theology may not be thus challenged, the remainder of this volume is incorporated in this extended work. The five distinctive ministries of the Holy Spirit to the believer are now to be considered in the following order: (a) regeneration, (b) the indwelling of the Holy Spirit, (c) the baptism with the Holy Spirit, (d) the sealing of the Holy Spirit, and (e) the filling with the Holy Spirit.[19]

Once again, Chafer appreciated the emphasis of the Keswick movement on the Holy Spirit but not the entire message of the movement.

Chafer's View of Sanctification Compared with Ryrie's
When comparing Chafer's view of sanctification with Ryrie's, it seems that they both share much in common. Like Chafer, Ryrie does not devote an entire chapter to sanctification.[20] He does share Chafer's basic categories. In

---

[19] Ibid., 103.
[20] Ryrie's views are summarized in Ryrie, *Basic Theology,* 442–43.

Basic Theology, Ryrie discusses the meaning of words related to sanctification with similar definitions (sanctify, saint, and holy). He describes sanctification in the similar categories of positional sanctification, experiential or progressive sanctification, and ultimate sanctification. He also cites similar agents of sanctification: the triune God and the believer who yields to the Holy Spirit.

Chafer's View of Sanctification Compared with Bock and Blaising's

Chafer and Ryrie use few pages to address sanctification. There is no indication of widespread substantial disagreement on their views. Bock and Blaising, however, prefer to focus on the communal aspects of sanctification as opposed to the individual ones.

In *Progressive Dispensationalism*, they make the following comparison between themselves and traditional dispensationalists:

> Earlier dispensationalists stressed the personal, individual aspect of Christianity exclusively. Their argument that one can only be born again personally, by personal faith in Christ, not by the actions of others apart from personal faith is sound, and practically all evangelicals would agree with this. There are many aspects of ministry built around this truth, but we shall not explore them here.
> Rather, we will explore the other aspects of ministry that flow from or are highlighted by the fact that the

church is a manifestation of a future kingdom in a special form in this dispensation. These relate to the *social ministry of the church.*[21]

As a result, some dispensationalists argue that the view of the present form of the kingdom inspires more social action rather than what they consider to be the negative view of traditional dispensationalism.

While this is an interesting contrast between progressive and essentialist dispensationalism, it is not an entirely accurate one. Stallard, in a paper that was given in response to a similar assertion by a progressive dispensationalist states:

> These simple facts point to the rather obvious truth that the root problems for race relations in this country transcend what view of dispensationalism one opts for. Does what view of dispensationalism one hold to really matter? Of course, it does. However, in trying to deal with such a profound, horrible, and long-standing sin problem within our own culture, it seems a bit simplistic to address the issue of the timing of the inauguration of the Messianic kingdom as a major player in the solution. To assert that the character of the present age is the real culprit, i.e., an overly pessimistic view of the Church Age, is the proverbial Band-Aid for cancer. As I read Bob's paper, I wondered that if we approach the topic in this way, will we be like those who, while the Titanic sinks, argue about what song the band is

---

[21] Blaising and Bock, *Progressive Dispensationalism*, 286.

playing? Racial reconciliation in particular and social action in general are too serious to try to solve at the level of the sub-points of our theological outline.[22]

Stallard's point is an exceptional one. The issue of social involvement is not necessarily decided by the difference between essentialist and progressive dispensationalism. Both essentialist and progressive dispensationalists are socially involved to varying degrees. A lack of social involvement is not an inevitable consequence of a traditional dispensationalist view of sanctification. As Augustine has said, you cannot judge the validity of a philosophy by the level of its abuse.

Stallard continues by showing that one should not adopt a progressive dispensational view of the inaugurated kingdom simply because of whatever social benefits may come:

> Fourth, I am somewhat surprised at Bob's statement that "traditional dispensational theology has not demanded social disengagement, but it has provided a theological loophole for those whose understanding of social ethics had been thrown out of balance by sin, controversy, and culture." There is a ring of truth to the statement that I cannot deny. There are always those who will take a theological point and abuse it. That will be true till Jesus comes. But his solution is grounded in the progressive dispensational attempt to recast the

---

[22] Mike Stallard, "An Essentialist Response to Robert A. Pyne's 'The New Man in an Immoral Society: Expectations between the Times'," (paper presented at the annual meeting of the Evangelical Theological Society, San Jose, CA, 20–22 November 1991), 3.

present age as the inaugurated form of the kingdom. The supposed model of reconciliation is a noble one. However, it is neither sufficient nor necessary.

I reject the idea that to prevent a theological loophole, one must revamp the original theological statement (in this case traditional dispensationalism's view of the present age). A host of significant examples shows the possible meaninglessness of such an exercise in general. Do I recast the teachings of Christ and Paul because their teachings have provided ample ammunition to those who wanted to justify slavery (e.g., see Ephesians 6, Philemon)? Should Reformed theologians recast their theology simply because some accuse them of anti-Semitism based upon their rejection of the present role of Jews as the nationally chosen race? Should Christians remodel their approach to evangelism and missions just because some Jews believe that the very fact of evangelism is anti-Semitic? Theological loopholes exist sometimes not because of bad theological emphases but because of the abuse of adherents or the misunderstandings of opponents.

While Stallard recognizes the potential abuse of the traditional dispensational view of the kingdom, he refuses to adjust his view of the kingdom without exegetical warrant:

> This all gets us back to the need to develop a social ethic on exegetical grounds before our theological system is put in place. I do not doubt that my progressive brothers are serious about exegesis and I only ask that my more traditionalist brothers would do the same. My

heartbeat (and part of why I accepted the invitation to come to this forum) is to help convince traditionalists of the great need for a social activism that is still subordinated to the primacy of the gospel of Christ. Contrary to what you might expect, I am 'optimistic' about the prospects (contrary to how a traditionalist is supposed to think about things in this age). However, I am 'pessimistic' (I'm back to my traditional pessimism) that dispensationalists as a whole will get on the same page to impact our culture, especially if traditional dispensational theology is cast as a theological loophole.[23]

Stallard's essentialist view disputes the progressive notion that the traditional dispensational view inevitably emphasizes a pessimistic view of the present age as opposed to an optimistic view. Neither view can claim a greater advantage on that account. As Stallard argues, the question of whether an inaugurated kingdom has taken place is made on an exegetical basis and not a utilitarian one.

Summary of Views of Sanctification

This evaluation of Chafer's view of sanctification demonstrates continuity with Ryrie. Both begin by defining the terms of sanctification. Both emphasize the positional, progressive, and ultimate aspects of sanctification. They both discuss the agents of sanctification. There is no indication of significant disagreement between progressive and traditional dispensationalists to that end. However, progressive

---

[23] Ibid., 5–6.

dispensationalists attempt to focus more on the communal aspects of sanctification. They do so on the basis of a belief in an inaugurated kingdom. As Stallard has argued, however, this is not an inevitable consequence of either traditional or progressive dispensationalism.

6
Chafer's Theological System: Israel and the Church

One critical doctrine that essentialist dispensationalists hold dear is the distinction between the church and Israel. Chafer espoused this view like many essentialist dispensationalists today. Like dispensationalists of his time, he did advocate two people of God with two distinct purposes. His distinction between the church and Israel was a result of his literal hermeneutic.

ISRAEL AND THE CHURCH

Chafer's View of Israel and the Church

Chafer's distinction between Israel and the church was heavily influenced by his literal hermeneutic, as this quote indicates:

> That Israel will yet return to her land and experience great national blessing is one of the Bible's most positive predictions—a forecast which yields to no fanciful notions for its interpretation. It must either be accepted in its literal form or ignored completely. Too often the

> latter is done. Men of course must ignore these Scriptures who deny any real distinction between Israel and the Church, for, as before declared, dispersion and regathering is utterly foreign to the Church. Upwards of fifty assertive passages declare that Israel will be regathered into their own land from this the third and final dispersion.[1]

Chafer believed that a failure to recognize the difference between Israel and the church was primarily a result of theological eisegesis and not a literal interpretation of the text. He believed that if someone was interpreting the New Testament and Old Testament literally, they would arrive at the same distinctions he did.

Chafer based this distinction on several arguments. One of his arguments is based on the nature of Christ's ministry while on earth:

> Probably no clearer evidence respecting the scope and purpose of Christ's first advent can be discovered than is indicated in His teaching, especially that of the major discourses. His ministry to Israel and to the Church are therein distinguished completely—to those not blinded by theological prejudice.[2]

Once again, Chafer believed that theological prejudice would be the main reason for not espousing this view.

---

[1] Chafer, *Systematic Theology*, vol. 7, 126.
[2] Ibid., 80.

Chafer also argued for the distinction based on his view of the national election of Israel and the individual election of members of the church:

> In its primary doctrinal meaning the word *call* [emphasis his] suggests an invitation from God to men. This meaning is extended to form a ground upon which the ones invited are designated *the called ones* [emphasis his]. The efficacious call of God is equivalent to His sovereign choice. Since there are two elect companies now in the world—Israel and the Church—these are alike seen as called of God. However, Israel's call is national while the call of those who comprise the Church is individual. The certainty of Israel's call is declared in the words, 'For the gifts and calling of God are without repentance' (Romans 11:29). Thus, Israel's blessing, which reaches into eternity to come, is guaranteed.[3]

As a result of this distinct calling, both groups had a distinct inheritance. The nation of Israel was an earthly people who could expect an earthly inheritance of the earthly blessings of the Old Testament. The church consisted of a heavenly people who had a heavenly inheritance awaiting them. Rather than trying to force unity as covenant theologians do, Chafer advocated two separate purposes for two separate groups because of his literal interpretation of the Bible:

---

[3] Ibid., 65.

> The dispensationalist does not create the great differences as he is sometimes accused of doing. The conflicting principles, such as may be found in the text of Scripture, are observable by all who penetrate deep enough to recognize the essential features of divine administration. Instead of creating the problems, the dispensationalist is actually the one who has a solution for them. If the ideals of an earthly people for long life in the land which God gave unto them (Exodus 20:12; Psalm 37:3, 11, 34; Matthew 5:5) does not articulate with the ideals of a heavenly people who, while on the earth, are but "strangers and pilgrims" and enjoined to be looking for and loving the imminent appearing of Christ (2 Timothy 4:8; Titus 2:13; 1 Peter 2:11), the problem is easily solved by the one whose system of interpretation will be proved rather than distressed by such distinctions. A plan of interpretation which, in defense of an ideal unity of the Bible, contends for a single divine purpose, ignores drastic contradictions, and is sustained only by occasional or accidental similarities, must be doomed to confusion when confronted with the many problems which such a system imposes on the text of Scripture, which problems are recognized by the dispensationalist only as he observes them in such a system as would create them.[4]

As a result, Chafer unapologetically argued for two separate people, with two separate purposes and ultimately two separate forms of inheritance.

---

[4] Ibid., 212.

Comparison with Ryrie

This view is not unlike many essentialist dispensationalists. Ryrie quotes Chafer in his discussion of the matter in his book *Dispensationalism*.[5] Ryrie ultimately concludes, "The apparent dichotomy between heavenly and earthly purposes means this: The earthly purpose of Israel of which dispensationalists speak concerns the yet unfulfilled national promises that will be fulfilled by Israel during the Millennium as they live on the earth in unresurrected bodies."[6] Likewise, Ryrie quotes Chafer in his discussion of the church as parenthesis.[7] Once again, this demonstrates continuity with respect to these key issues as opposed to discontinuity.

Comparison with Bock and Blaising

One of the major issues that Bock and Blaising point out regarding classical dispensationalists is the "essential dualism" in the idea of redemption. They call it "the most important feature of classical dispensationalism."[8] This seems overstated, especially in light of the consistent focus on topics like literal interpretation, the separation of the church and Israel, the future kingdom, etc. According to Bock and Blaising this dual form of redemption relates to two different purposes: one earthly and the other heavenly. According to Blaising and Bock, the earthly purpose is to release the earth from corruption and decay in order to restore a humanity free from

---

[5] See Charles Caldwell Ryrie, *Dispensationalism*, revised and expanded ed. (Chicago, IL: Moody Press, 1995), 136–37.
[6] Ibid., 136.
[7] Ibid., 150.
[8] Blaising and Bock, *Progressive Dispensationalism*, 23.

death and sin.⁹ Without citing a reference, Blaising and Bock speak of early dispensationalists who argued that the earth will be repopulated forever. According to Bock and Blaising, the heavenly purpose is regarding the transdispensational heavenly people who are in the presence of the Lord whose hope lies in the future resurrection.

According to Blaising and Bock, there is significant discontinuity between the classical view and the revised view on this issue:

> The most important revision introduced by the dispensationalists of the 50s and 60s was their abandonment of the eternal dualism of heavenly and earthly peoples. They did not believe that there would be an eternal destination between one humanity in heaven and another in the new earth. Consequently, they dropped the forms of the heavenly and earthly peoples. Instead they reworked the dualism in more of an organized sense (closer to the meaning of the term dispensation). There were simply two groups of people. Not heavenly versus earthly, but those represented by Israel and the church.¹⁰

It is important to note that although Chafer does use the terms *heavenly* and *earthly* people (see volume 4 page 12 for example), he also clearly addresses the church and Israel. Ryrie even alludes to his terminology. As a result, the alleged

---

⁹ Ibid.
¹⁰ Ibid., 31–32.

differences that make up such a significant revision in Bock and Blaising's view seem overstated.

In contrast to the other views, Bock and Blaising state their own view:

> Progressive dispensationalists agree with revised (and classical) dispensationalists that God's work with Israel and Gentile nations in the past dispensation looks forward to the redemption of humanity in its political and cultural aspects. Consequently, there is a plan for Israel and for other nations in the eternal plan of God.
> On the other hand, Progressive dispensationalists believe that the church is a vital part of this *very same plan of redemption* [emphasis his]. The appearance of the church does not signal a secondary redemption plan, either to be fulfilled in heaven apart from the new earth or in an elite class of Jews and Gentiles who are forever distinguished from the rest of redeemed humanity. Indeed, the church today is a revelation of spiritual blessings which *all the redeemed* [emphasis his] will share in spite of their ethnic and national differences.
> Consequently, progressive dispensationalism advocates a *holistic and unified view* [emphasis his] of eternal salvation. God will save humankind in its ethnic and national purity. But, He will bless it with the same salvation given to all without distinction, the same, not only in justification and regeneration, but also in sanctification by the indwelling Holy Spirit. These blessings will come to all without distinction through

Jesus Christ, the king of Israel and all the nations of redeemed humanity.[11]

Thus, Bock and Blaising advocate their position because they believe it gives a more holistic and unified view of eternal salvation for all mankind.

It must be stated that both classical and essentialist dispensationalism shared a holistic and unified purpose of God. This is the essence of Ryrie's third point on the doxological purpose of God. In essence, he was arguing that the central unifying theme is God's glory as revealed in his distinct purposes. God is not only glorified in individual redemption but also in His sovereign plan for man, angels, the earth, Israel, and the church. Bock's statement seems to argue for a unifying theme in justification and sanctification while ignoring the overall unifying theme of God's glory. He focuses primarily on individual salvation and sanctification without recognizing God's overall purpose to glorify Himself in many different ways.

One excellent article that deals with this issue from an essentialist perspective is "Prophetic Hope in the Writings of Arno C. Gaebelein: A Possible Demonstration of the Doxological Purpose of Biblical History."[12] Not only is this article important for emphasizing continuity between the classical and revised view of God's purposes for Israel and the church, it also addresses the central unifying theme of the Bible from a traditional dispensationalist perspective. In this

---

[11] Ibid., 47–48.
[12] Mike Stallard, "Prophetic Hope in the Writings of Arno C. Gaebelein: A Possible Demonstration of the Doxological Purpose of Biblical History," *Journal of Ministry and Theology* 2, no. 2 (Fall 1998): 190–211.

article, Stallard explains the fact of unity in diversity in Ryrie's third point as follows:

> Further, it is possible to see the doxological purpose to biblical history as a corollary to the distinction between Israel and the Church. Although the multi-track approach to biblical history as cited in Gaebelein's five-fold presentation above is clear, the primary distinction in the list is that between Israel and the Church. Simply put, the dispensationalist is open to the diversity which the biblical text yields because of his belief in a great sovereign God who can coordinate multiple tracks in His will and way. By implication the covenant theologian may not be so open to such diversity since he has a tendency to unify every aspect at the point of individual election.[13]

Thus, Stallard points out that the essentialist position is actually more unified for the entire Bible because it recognizes God's sovereignty in all aspects of God's reign and not just individual election as covenant theologians do.

With respect to the distinction between Israel and the church, progressive dispensationalism moves toward a notion of believing in one people of God.[14] They believe that this is true in an already sense through the church and ultimately in a not yet sense after the millennium. By arguing that the church

---

[13] Ibid., 207.

[14] For an assessment of the Progressive Dispensationalist teaching of one people of God see John Brumett, "Does Progressive Dispensationalism Teach a Posttribulational Rapture?—Part I," *Conservative Theological Journal* 2, no. 5 (June 1998): 194.

fulfills covenants that were originally given to Israel (even if in a limited already sense), the distinction between the church and Israel is further diminished. Thus, while there is significant agreement between Chafer and Ryrie on this matter, the discontinuity with progressive dispensationalism is significant.

7
Chafer's Theological System: Covenants

CHAFER'S VIEW OF THE COVENANTS

Closely related to the distinct people of God was Chafer's view of the covenants. His understanding of their purpose and expected fulfillment was largely based on his literal hermeneutic and his distinction between the church and Israel. This section reviews the twelve covenants that Chafer discussed and his belief in how they would be fulfilled. His incorporation of the theological covenants of covenant theology (covenant of redemption, covenant of works, and covenant of grace) is different from most modern-day essentialist dispensationalists' lists of Biblical covenants. Many, although not all, essentialist dispensationalists disagree with his distinction between two new covenants. Most essentialist dispensationalists, however, agree with his beliefs on the future fulfillment of the Abrahamic, Palestinian, Davidic, and new covenants.

Chafer listed twelve covenants in his discussion on this topic: (1) the covenant of redemption, (2) the covenant of works, (3) the covenant of grace, (4) the Edenic covenant, (5) the

Adamic covenant, (6) the Noahic covenant, (7) the Abrahamic covenant, (8) the Mosaic covenant, (9) the Palestinian covenant, (10) the Davidic covenant, (11) the new covenant for the church, (12) and the new covenant for Israel.[1] Most essentialist dispensationalists would find this list interesting for several reasons. First, Chafer is one of the few dispensational theologians who integrated covenants from covenant theology with the dispensational covenants. This is especially interesting in light of his reliance on the Bible alone for establishing doctrine. Regarding the covenant of redemption Chafer writes, "This covenant rests upon but slight revelation. It is rather sustained largely by the fact that it seems both reasonable and inevitable."[2] Thus, Chafer borrowed some concepts from his Presbyterian upbringing and inserted them into his dispensational framework with little or no explanation on how he justified this Biblically.

One other concept that many essentialist dispensationalists might find interesting is his concept of two new covenants. Chafer describes the new covenant for the church as that "which incorporates every promise of saving and keeping grace for those of the present age who believe. Its many blessings are either possessions or positions in Christ."[3] He describes the new covenant for Israel as that which "is 'new' in the sense that it supersedes as a rule of life the Mosaic Covenant that Israel broke, but it does not alter or conflict with the Palestinian Covenant, the Abrahamic Covenant, or the Davidic Covenant. Its blessings are fourfold and all yet future, though assured unconditionally on the unfailing faithfulness of

---

[1] Chafer, *Systematic Theology*, vol. 1, 42–43.
[2] Ibid., 42.
[3] Ibid., 43.

God."[4] This distinction was heavily influenced by Chafer's literal interpretation and his strong distinction between the church and Israel. While not all essentialist dispensationalists advocate two new covenants, some do agree with Chafer that there are two new covenants described in the Bible. Ryrie, for instance, bases his argument on the lack of a definite article in Hebrews 9:15 and 12:24.[5]

While not all dispensationalists agree with Chafer's list of covenants (which includes two new covenants), many agree with his view of the Abrahamic and Davidic covenants. Chafer says, "The Abrahamic covenant records Jehovah's sovereign purpose in, through, and for Abraham. The covenant is unconditional in that no obligation is imposed upon Abraham; he contributes nothing, but rather is the recipient of all that Jehovah proposed to do for him. While this covenant (cf. Gen. 12:1–3; 13:14–17; 15:4–7; 17:1–8) provided personal blessings and great honor to Abraham, its more important features reach out in two other directions, namely, that of Abraham's seed and that of the land of promise."[6] Like many essentialist dispensationalists, Chafer considered the Abrahamic covenant to be unconditional, and ultimate fulfillment of all aspects would occur in the millennium. The descendants of Abraham would receive an everlasting nation and an everlasting possession of the land.

---

[4] Ibid.
[5] Ryrie, *Dispensationalism*, 174.
[6] Chafer, *Systematic Theology*, vol. 5, 317.

RYRIE'S VIEW OF THE COVENANTS

As previously mentioned, there are many similarities between Chafer's view of the covenants and the essentialist view. However, there are some key differences with respect to the number of covenants. This section describes Ryrie's view of the covenants as compared to Chafer's.

Ryrie focuses his attention in *Basic Theology* discussing the Abrahamic and Davidic covenants. His view of the Abrahamic covenant is pretty consistent with Chafer's:

> Premillennialism insists that all the provisions of the Abrahamic Covenant must be fulfilled since the covenant was made without conditions. Much of the covenant has already been fulfilled and fulfilled literally; therefore, what remains to be fulfilled will also be fulfilled literally. This brings the focus on the yet-unfulfilled land promise. Though the nation Israel occupied part of the territory promised in the covenant, she has never yet occupied all of it and certainly not eternally as the covenant promised. Therefore, there must be a time in the future when Israel will do so, and for the premillennialist this will be in the coming millennial kingdom. Thus, the Abrahamic Covenant gives strong support for premillennial eschatology.[7]

Thus, Ryrie focuses on the unconditional nature of the Abrahamic covenant and its fulfillment in the millennium.

---

[7] Ryrie, *Basic Theology*, 530.

Ryrie also has a view of the Davidic covenant that is consistent with Chafer's.[8] He argues that the provisions for David were descendants and a kingdom. He believes that Solomon was promised a temple, throne, and punishment. Ryrie argues that the Davidic covenant is unconditional and will be fulfilled in the eschaton.

As previously mentioned, Ryrie's view of two new covenants is similar to Chafer's. In his book, *The Basis of the Premillennial Faith* he writes, "The induction that there are two new covenants strengthens the premillennial position and does not permit the amillennialist to say that the Church is fulfilling Israel's promises."[9] However, he later reflected a change of position in his definition of the new covenant in the Wycliffe Bible Encyclopedia[10] only to change it back again when he wrote the revised and expanded edition of *Dispensationalism*.[11]

BLAISING AND BOCK'S VIEW OF THE COVENANTS

Blaising and Bock do not make significant distinctions in identifying the Biblical covenants. However, they do argue for differences in how they define the covenants and their fulfillment. This section describes both aspects of Blaising and Bock's view of the covenants.

---

[8] See his discussion in Ryrie, *Basic Theology*, 532–534.
[9] Charles C. Ryrie, *The Basis of the Premillennial Faith* (Dubuque, IA: ECS Ministries, 2005) 104.
[10] Cf. Charles C. Ryrie, "Covenant, New," in *The Wycliffe Bible Encyclopedia*, ed. Charles F. Pfeiffer, Howard Frederic Vos, and John Rea (Chicago, IL: Moody Press, 1975), 391–392.
[11] Ryrie, *Dispensationalism*, 174.

With regard to identification of the covenants, there are some differences in their identification in comparison with Ryrie and Chafer. Like Ryrie, Blaising and Bock do not include the covenant of works, covenant of grace, or covenant of redemption that Chafer included. They also do not believe in two new covenants and recognize some changes in that perspective by Ryrie and Walvoord. They identify the following covenants: the Noahic covenant, the Abrahamic covenant, the Mosaic covenant, the Davidic covenant and the new covenant. The two notable omissions from the traditional lists given by some essentialist dispensationalists are the Adamic covenant and the Palestinian covenant.

The major difference between progressive dispensationalism and traditional dispensationalism is the fulfillment of the covenants. Blaising and Bock write:

> Progressive dispensationalism offers a more unified view of the biblical covenants than earlier dispensationalism. The Abrahamic covenant is seen as the foundation for all the other covenants ... The new covenant is *the form* [their emphasis] in which the Abrahamic covenant has been inaugurated in this dispensation and will be fulfilled in full in the future. The Davidic covenant is both an aspect of Abrahamic blessing and *the means* [their emphasis] by which the blessings are now inaugurated and will be bestowed in full.[12]

---

[12] Blaising and Bock, *Progressive Dispensationalism*, 53.

Thus, while many essentialist dispensationalists agree that the Abrahamic covenant is the main covenant from which the other covenants are related, they do not agree with the implications of this notion that Blaising and Bock advocate. This is especially true of the alleged "already-not-yet" implications of the covenant fulfillment. Blaising and Bock elaborate on this concept in another section of their book:

> It is possible to get fulfillment "now" in some texts, while noting that "not yet" fulfillment exists in other passages. In fact, in some texts fulfillment can be initial or partial as opposed to being final and total. As a result, one can speak of inaugurated eschatology without denying either what the Old Testament indicates about the future, earthly kingdom or what the New Testament asserts about the arrival of the kingdom as part of fulfillment in the first coming of Jesus.[13]

This statement is a strong departure from the traditional views of Chafer and Ryrie. For Chafer and Ryrie, fulfillment implies that all aspects of the promise were realized in their entirety. However, Bock and Blaising lend a meaning to that term that is inconsistent with the traditional dispensational views.

---

[13] Ibid., 97–98.

8
Chafer's Theological System: Dispensations

CHAFER'S DISPENSATIONS

This section discusses Chafer's list of seven dispensations. Special attention is given to how he defines a dispensation and how he identifies the purpose of a dispensation. Chafer's view of dispensations does not depart too much from the essentialist position today.

Chafer defines a dispensation as, "Translated from the word οἰκονομία, meaning primarily *stewardship*, a dispensation is a specific, divine economy, a commitment from God to man of a responsibility to discharge that which God has appointed him."[1] This is not too different from Ryrie who defines a dispensation as a "distinguishable economy in the outworking of God's purpose."[2] Chafer qualifies how they are to be identified when he writes:

> As a time measurement, a dispensation is a period which is identified by its relation to some particular

---
[1] Chafer, *Systematic Theology*, vol. 7, page 122.
[2] Ryrie, *Dispensationalism*, 28.

purpose of God—a purpose to be accomplished within that period. The earlier dispensations, being so far removed in point of time from the present, are not as clearly defined as are the later dispensations. For this reason, Bible expositors are not always agreed regarding the precise features of the more remote periods.[3]

Ryrie seems to disconnect the concept of dispensation from the time measurement when he writes: "A dispensation is basically the arrangement involved, not the time involved, and a proper definition takes this into account. However, there is no reason for great alarm if a definition does ascribe time to a dispensation."[4] Thus, Chafer's definition does not differ substantially from the essentialist position as described by Ryrie. Chafer emphasizes the time element and bases his definition more on the word *dispensation* than Ryrie does. Despite this, they are quite similar in their approach.

Chafer considers an understanding of the dispensations to be essential to good hermeneutics:

> Doubtless the key to the understanding of the Bible is the recognition of the specific purpose of God in each of the succeeding ages of human history. Dispensational distinctions have always engendered true expository preaching, while Covenant Theology has tended toward a closing and slighting of the Word of God.[5]

---

[3] Chafer, *Systematic Theology*, vol. 1, page 40.
[4] Ryrie, *Dispensationalism*, 28.
[5] Chafer, *Systematic Theology*, vol. 7, 45.

Chafer relates the covenants and dispensations together as illustrating God's overall purpose:

> The Bible demonstrates its authority by proposing a divine program which God alone could complete. To a considerable degree this program has been executed. Apart from such an all-comprehensive plan, how could Jehovah's everlasting and all-inclusive covenants with Abraham, David, Israel, and the Church—in which He assumes a determining direction over all generations of human life—be interpreted?[6]

Ultimately, Chafer considers the covenants to be essential to dispensational interpretation. He criticizes those who "disregard or ignore the earthly covenants and promises; they spiritualize or vaporize the vast body of Scripture bearing on the Davidic Throne and Kingdom; they present no specific reason as to why Christ was born as the Son of David; and they recognize no earthly glory or purpose in His second advent. According to their system, Christ comes again to end the world, but, unfortunately for these conceptions, the world does not end then or ever."[7]

Chafer identifies seven dispensations in his system. He lists the "obvious dispensational divisions" as: (1) the dispensation of innocence, (2) the dispensation of conscience, (3) the dispensation of human government, (4) the dispensation of promise, (5) the dispensation of the Law, (6) the dispensation

---

[6] Lewis Sperry Chafer, "Part 5: Bibliology," *Bibliotheca Sacra* 95, no. 378 (April–June 1938): 155–56.
[7] Chafer, "Dispensationalism," 448–49.

of grace, (7) and the dispensation of kingdom rule.⁸ Many essentialist dispensationalists also have seven dispensations.

Chafer's definitions of each dispensation are also an important part of this discussion. Chafer defines the dispensation of innocence as that "which extended from the creation to the fall of Adam. The time is unrevealed; Adam's divine commission in that period and his failure indicate the course and end of the divine intention within that era."⁹ He describes the dispensation of conscience as that "which extended from Adam's fall to the flood, in which age conscience was, apparently, the dominating feature of human life on the earth and the basis of man's relationship with God."¹⁰ He considers the dispensation of human government to be that "which extended from the flood to the call of Abraham" and "is characterized by the committing of self-government to men, and is terminated by the introduction of a new divine purpose."¹¹ He describes the dispensation of promise as the "time from the call of Abraham to the giving and acceptance of the Mosaic Law at Sinai."¹² During this dispensation Chafer believes "the divine promise alone sustains Abraham and his posterity. While Hebrews 11:13, 39 refer to Old Testament saints generally in that no major Old Testament promise was realized during its own period, these passages are specifically true of those who lived within the age of promise. That Abraham lived by divine promise is a theme of both

---

⁸ Chafer, *Systematic Theology*, vol. 1, 40–41.
⁹ Ibid., 40.
¹⁰ Ibid.
¹¹ Ibid.
¹² Ibid.

Testaments."[13] According to Chafer, the dispensation of the Law extended "from the giving of the Law of Jehovah by Moses and its acceptance by Israel at Sinai (Ex. 19:3–31:18)" and "it continued as the authoritative government of God over His people Israel and thus characterized that age until it ended with the death of Christ [although he also includes the Tribulation as well]."[14] Chafer argues that the dispensation of grace covers the time period "from the death of Christ until His return to receive His Bride."[15] According to Chafer, this dispensation is "characterized by grace in the sense that in this age God, who has always acted in grace toward any and all of the human family whom He has blessed, is now making a specific heavenly demonstration of His grace by and through the whole company of Jews and Gentiles who are saved by grace through faith in Christ. These are a heavenly people who, because their citizenship is in heaven, are removed both by resurrection and translation from the earth when their elect number is completed."[16] According to Chafer, the dispensation of kingdom rule "continues from the second advent of Christ for a thousand years and ends with the creation of a new heaven and a new earth. It is characterized by the facts that Satan is bound, the covenants of Israel are fulfilled, creation is delivered from its bondage, and the Lord Himself will reign over the earth and on the throne of His father David."[17]

---

[13] Ibid.
[14] Ibid.
[15] Ibid.
[16] Ibid.
[17] Ibid.

COMPARISON OF DISPENSATIONS WITH RYRIE

The list of dispensations is not substantially different from other essentialist dispensationalists. Ryrie basically has the same list as Chafer with slightly different titles.[18] The only minor difference is that Chafer places the tribulation period under the dispensation of the Law while Ryrie places it at the end of the dispensation of Grace.[19] Once again, Ryrie's number of dispensations demonstrates continuity with Chafer instead of discontinuity.[20] For the most part, with the exception of the inclusion of the tribulation in the dispensation of the Law, few essentialist dispensationalists argue with Chafer's view of the dispensations. They might, however, prefer that he focus less on the time and events of each dispensation and more on the person, responsibility, and tests that characterize them.

COMPARISON OF DISPENSATIONS WITH BLAISING AND BOCK

While there are some minor disagreements with respect to dispensations between Chafer and Ryrie, they are not quite as significant as differences between Chafer and progressive dispensationalists. Blaising and Bock list four dispensations in Biblical history: the Patriarchal (which is until Sinai), the Mosaic (which is up to the Messiah's ascension), the Ecclesial

---

[18] See Ryrie, *Dispensationalism*, 51–57.
[19] Ibid., 49–51.
[20] It must be noted that Ryrie does not necessarily represent all essentialist dispensationalists. Some may have more or fewer dispensations that he does. However, since he was the first person to identify the essentials of dispensationalism, his opinion is especially helpful.

(which is up to Messiah's return), and the Zionic (which includes the millennial kingdom and the eternal state).[21] They base this on the principles of "simplicity and flexibility."[22] They base their distinctions on their complementary hermeneutical assumptions that the New Covenant has been inaugurated:

> As we have seen, transition from the past dispensation to the present involves covenantal change. The past dispensation was characterized by the Mosaic covenant; the present dispensation is characterized by certain blessings of the new covenant which have appeared in an inaugurated form. Both dispensations are ways of relating the promises of the Patriarchal and Davidic Covenants (given in a yet earlier dispensation).[23]

Thus, essentialist dispensationalism demonstrates continuity with Chafer's and Ryrie's dispensations. On the other hand, progressive dispensationalism shows discontinuity with Chafer in its definition and identification of dispensations.

---

[21] Blaising and Bock, *Progressive Dispensationalism*, 123.
[22] Ibid., 122.
[23] Ibid., 125.

9

Chafer's Theological System: Eschatology

CHAFER'S ESCHATOLOGY

This final section of Chafer's theology describes his eschatology. Special attention is given to his view of the rapture, tribulation, millennium, and eternal state. This section once again emphasizes the continuity of Chafer's eschatology with essentialist dispensationalism.

Chafer does not discuss the rapture extensively in his *Systematic Theology*. He discusses the millennium in far more detail. With respect to the rapture, his focus is primarily on the nature of the body when it occurs. He describes a time when "the whole company who comprise the Church and each one in particular, or individually, will be so changed that the company will be the glorified Bride of the Lamb."[1] Chafer expresses belief in a pretribulational rapture:

> In general, those who contend that the Church will experience the tribulation assert that all believers—

---

[1] Lewis Sperry Chafer, "Populating the Third Heaven," *Bibliotheca Sacra* 108, no. 430 (April–June 1951): 151.

> spiritual and unspiritual—will enter that period of suffering, though there are those believing in a partial rapture who assert that the Church will be divided and the spiritual element, which always includes those who advance this notion, will go directly to heaven, while the unspiritual will suffer for their sins in the tribulation. This constitutes a Protestant purgatory. The answer to all such conceptions is the recognition of the truth that, when members of this sinful race go to heaven, it is not on the ground of their own merit, but only through the merit of Christ. It is to be remembered that each believer is already perfectly justified forever (Rom. 5:1; 8:30, 33–34) and this wholly within the range of divine justice (Rom. 3:26). Thus, the contention that the Church will enter or pass through the tribulation becomes an insult to, and unbelief towards, the measureless grace of God in Christ.[2]

Chafer's primary Biblical justification for his pretribulational view comes from a discussion on Revelation 3:10 in his *Systematic Theology*.[3]

Like most dispensationalists, Chafer distinguishes between the millennial kingdom and heaven. For instance, he says:

> It should be remembered that the millennium is not heaven. On the contrary, it is to be characterized by a limited amount of evil which Christ the King will judge perfectly and immediately (Isa. 11:1–16). Neither is it

---

[2] Chafer, *Systematic Theology*, vol. 4, 365–66.
[3] Ibid., 369–71.

that new earth which God will yet create (Isa. 65:17; 66:22; 2 Pet. 3:13; Rev. 21:1) for therein righteousness dwells, which is something not true of the millennium.[4]

Chafer considers the message of the millennial kingdom to be consistent with the portrayal in the Old Testament:

> Continuing this major theme of Old Testament prophecy, the New Testament again adds many details. The kingdom teachings of Christ, addressed to Israel as recorded in the Synoptic Gospels, portray the character and glory of that coming age, while the Apostle John reveals its duration to be a period of one thousand years (Rev. 20:4, 6).[5]

He also considers it to literally be one thousand years:

> The Scriptures indicate yet another extended age to follow the present one—that of the kingdom on the earth, and it is to extend at least one thousand years. During this time it is clearly predicted that there will be two kinds of humanity on the earth, the Jews and such Gentiles as are chosen of God to share the kingdom with Israel. Thus, it is revealed that the present age is the only one in which the Christian dwells on the earth.[6]

As previously mentioned in a letter from December 1944, Chafer said that the "premillennial, dispensational

---

[4] Ibid., vol. 7, 238.
[5] Ibid., vol. 4, 389.
[6] Chafer, "Populating the Third Heaven," 139.

interpretation is the only one true to the Bible."[7] This issue was extremely important for Chafer as it is for most dispensationalists.

With respect to heaven, Chafer has some unique views. Consistent with his view of the eternal distinction between Israel and the Church, Chafer argues that Christians will populate the third heaven:

> The Scriptures indicate that there are three heavens. Direct reference is made to the third heaven in 2 Corinthians 12:2, and it is evident that there cannot be a third without a first and a second also. It is credible, and no doubt true, that the first heaven comprises the air space surrounding the earth, for reference is made to the birds of the heavens and the clouds of the heavens. It seems as likely that the second heaven includes the entire solar system, as reference is made to the stars of the heavens. The location of the third heaven has never been determined in any way whatever. However, it certainly exists ... The Scriptures indicate yet another extended age to follow the present one—that of the kingdom on the earth, and it is to extend at least one thousand years. During this time it is clearly predicted that there will be two kinds of humanity on the earth, the Jews and such Gentiles as are chosen of God to share the kingdom with Israel. Thus it is revealed that the present age is the only one in which the Christian dwells on the earth ... God has in all four orders of

---

[7] Lewis Sperry Chafer, *The Lewis Sperry Chafer Papers* (Jamestown, NC: Schnappsburg University Press), microform.

intelligences in the universe which He has caused to exist, namely, the angels, the Gentiles, the Jews and the Christians. There is more difference between a Christian and a Gentile or Jew than there is between an angel and a Gentile or Jew. If this statement seems extreme, it is due to the fact that many do not understand just what a Christian is. As a special creation of God, the Christian far exceeds any of the angels. Things are said to be true of the Christian, certainly, which are never said of any angel. This fact will be seen as the pages to follow are pursued. The purpose of this thesis is to set forth what a Christian really is so far as can now be clearly stated, and that it is God's purpose in calling out such as the Christians to populate the third heaven.[8]

Chafer argues that this relates to the divine purpose as follows:

In concluding this particular thesis, it may be restated that the present divine purpose is that of "bringing many sons unto glory" (Heb. 2:10) and of fitting them to be dwellers in the third heaven. To this end they are mightily changed from the present fallen estate of men on earth, are forgiven all sin, constituted actual sons of God, clothed in the righteousness of God, perfected forever, and justified. They are yet to have a body like Christ's glorious body and to be conformed to His image. Their perfection is to be of such an exalted degree that they are to serve as the bride of Christ, in which He will eternally delight.

---

[8] Chafer, "Populating the Third Heaven," 139–40.

Even in this world the saved ones are given the perfect standing before God of Christ Himself and are therefore expected to walk worthy of such perfection, even to "shew forth the praises of him who hath called you out of darkness into his marvellous [sic] light."[9]

Thus, Chafer said that the key hope for the heavenly people was their future state in heaven.

COMPARISON WITH RYRIE'S ESCHATOLOGY

Ryrie's eschatology is fairly similar to Chafer's. His discussion on the rapture is much more extensive than Chafer's. However, like Chafer, he believes in a pretribulational rapture.[10] He also holds a premillennial position on the kingdom.[11] His discussion of the resurrection does not seem to make the same distinction of the eternal destiny of the earthly and heavenly people.[12] Thus, there appears to be a great deal of continuity between Ryrie and Chafer with respect to eschatology in spite of their minor differences.

---

[9] Ibid., 269.
[10] For more information, see Ryrie, *Basic Theology*, 557–68.
[11] See Ibid., 522–24.
[12] Ibid., 603–5.

COMPARISON WITH
BOCK AND BLAISING'S ESCHATOLOGY

Up until now, the key distinction of Bock and Blaising has been how much of eschatology has already been realized. Their already-not-yet complementary hermeneutic is a departure from the completely futurist eschatology of Ryrie and Chafer. Bock and Blaising claim to espouse a pretribulational rapture.[13] However, some question whether the suppositions of progressive dispensationalism logically results in a posttribulational rapture.[14]

One major difference between traditional dispensationalism and progressive dispensationalism is in how to interpret Revelation. Some progressive dispensationalists do not interpret several key passages literally in light of the apocalyptic nature of the book.[15] Some utilize the complementary hermeneutic to argue for an immediate fulfillment in John's time as some preterists do in an already sense but a view similar to the futurist in the not yet sense.[16] This may once again reflect the tendency of progressive dispensationalists to seek a compromise between two

---

[13] Blaising and Bock, *Progressive Dispensationalism*, 317.
[14] See Brumett, "Does Progressive Dispensationalism Teach a Posttribulational Rapture?—Part I": 191–203. Also see John Brumett, "Does Progressive Dispensationalism Teach a Posttribulational Rapture? Part II," *Conservative Theological Journal* 2 (September 1998): 319–32.
[15] See especially D. Brent Sandy, *Plowshares & Pruning Hooks: Rethinking the Language of Biblical Prophecy and Apocalyptic* (Downers Grove, IL: InterVarsity Press, 2002) 103–194.
[16] See especially C. Marvin Pate, "A Progressive Dispensational View of Revelation," in *Four Views on the Book of Revelation*, ed. C. Marvin Pate, (Grand Rapids, MI: Zondervan Publishing House, 1998), 135–75.

competing systems. These changes represent a significant departure from the eschatology of Ryrie and Chafer.

SUMMARY

This chapter discusses Chafer's theology. His contributions in the area of theology are significant. Chafer is one of the key theologians that recovered the free grace doctrine in soteriology. His view of sanctification emphasizes the power of the Holy Spirit in the life of the believer. Although his inclusion of the Covenants of Works, Grace, and Redemption in his list of covenants is unique among dispensationalists, his view of the distinction between Israel and the church as well as the dispensations is pretty consistent with essentialist dispensationalism. Chafer's view of the rapture and the millennium is also consistent with an essentialist dispensationalist view. However, his views on all of these issues have significant differences with those of the progressive dispensationalist camp.

10
Chafer's Contributions To Dispensationalism

This chapter discusses Chafer's unique contributions to dispensationalism. Chafer contributes significantly to dispensationalism, especially in his extensive writing, his unique systematization of dispensational truths, his mentoring of key figures in the movement, and his establishment of Dallas Theological Seminary.[1] This chapter elaborates on those key contributions.

On September 22, 1952, Homer A. Kent wrote Dr. Walvoord to inform him of the following resolution that was passed unanimously by the faculty of Grace Theological Seminary in Winona Lake, Indiana:

> Whereas God in His providence has seen fit to remove from the scenes of the earth one of His choicest saints, be it resolved that we of Grace Theological Seminary recognize with grateful appreciation the sterling

---

[1] These four categories of contributions are taken from Robert Green, "Lewis Sperry Chafer and Dallas Theological Seminary," (Baptist Bible Seminary, 2004), 39–41.

Christian character of Dr. Lewis Sperry Chafer, his uncompromising stand for "the faith once for all delivered unto the saints," his far-reaching contributions in the field of Christian education especially as a teacher and president of Dallas Theological Seminary, his outstanding writing ministry attested by numerous books and countless articles in which he held aloft the torch of divine truth in these days of spiritual declension, and, in short, his faithfulness as a minister of the Lord Jesus Christ in the pulpit, classroom, and on the lecture platform, as well as in the administrative affairs of the church. We are profoundly grateful for his fellowship in the things of God and realize that we have been made richer in the realm of our Christian experience by reason of his distinctive leadership. His homegoing leaves us with a sense of great loss, but we have been inspired by his victorious ministry through many years and thus are better able to contend for the faith in the days that remain to us until that great day when we shall meet in the Glory.[2]

This resolution is representative of several of the ways Chafer impacted many people in his time on the earth. This resolution recognizes the aspects of his contributions that this chapter endeavors to examine.

---

[2] Lewis Sperry Chafer, *The Lewis Sperry Chafer Papers* (Jamestown, NC: Schnappsburg University Press), microform.

CHAFER'S WRITING

Despite never completing his college education, Chafer was a prolific writer.[3] Clarence Mason wrote in a letter to Dallas Theological Seminary after learning of Chafer's death, "When one thinks of the written and spoken ministry of Dr. Chafer, quite apart from the Seminary, one is amazed at the prodigious amount of work accomplished by a man so frail."[4] While his books often stirred up controversy among evangelicals, they provided an important voice for the dispensational movement. Not only that, but Chafer served as an example to the Dallas Theological faculty propelling them to be prolific writers. His message would live on long after he was gone.

CHAFER'S SYSTEMATIZATION
OF DISPENSATIONAL TRUTHS

Of all his works, *Systematic Theology* is perhaps the most important contribution to dispensationalism. The depth, breadth, and exposure that the book had, made it a great feat in its time. In his review of the fourth edition Walvoord said:

> The occasion of the fourth printing of the eight-volume work in *Systematic Theology* by Lewis Sperry Chafer is a precedent-shattering record in contemporary theological literature. It is most unusual for any

---

[3] See pages 12–13 of this paper for a summary of some of Chafer's significant works.
[4] Chafer, *The Lewis Sperry Chafer Papers.*

systematic theology in our day to attract much interest. The fact that an eight-volume work has had such public demand and such widespread attention is most significant .... Reasons for its popularity are not difficult to find. *Systematic Theology* presents in wider scope than ever before attempted the whole realm of Biblical theology from the conservative and premillennial standpoint.[5]

This statement certainly demonstrates the importance of this book in the dispensational history. Chafer's *Systematic Theology* clearly defines many key dispensational beliefs and gives clarity to the entire dispensational system.

CHAFER'S CONTRIBUTIONS AS A MENTOR

As a mentor, Chafer also made a significant impact on many dispensational leaders. Men like Walvoord and Pentecost all learned from him. Everett F. Harrison remarked about him in a letter written on August 28, 1952:

> His teaching gift was remarkable. I can still recall things I heard at his lips thirty years ago. He had a great capacity for friendship, possessed such a genuine interest in young men studying for the ministry that they were complimented to be called "one of the boys."

---

[5] John F. Walvoord, "A Review of Lewis Sperry Chafer's 'Systematic Theology' Fourth Edition," *Bibliotheca Sacra* 111, no. 442 (April–June 1954): 169.

Many will be thanking God in these days that they were permitted to come under His teaching and influence.[6]

John Davis of Rutger's University remarked: "Dr. Chafer's life influenced us more than any other person with whom we have ever come in contact. He truly was a great man, and I know your institution is going to miss him sorely. We only express the hope that God will select some other worthy Christian to take his place."[7] Ironically, God did choose someone to take Lewis Sperry Chafer's place: his protégé John Walvoord.

DALLAS THEOLOGICAL SEMINARY

One of the most significant contribution Chafer made to the history of dispensationalism was the founding of Dallas Theological Seminary. This small school symbolized a hope of training future dispensational leaders. This was accomplished in the training of men like Charles Ryrie, J. Dwight Pentecost, Charles Swindoll, Tony Evans, Tommy Nelson, and many others. Dallas Theological Seminary faculty have published numerous books on a wide variety of topics.

SUMMARY

This chapter endeavors to demonstrate the significant contributions that Chafer made to dispensationalism. His writing, his systematization of dispensational truths, his ability to mentor, and the founding of Dallas Theological Seminary are the most significant ones. His life can be

---

[6] Chafer, *The Lewis Sperry Chafer Papers*.
[7] Ibid.

summarized in a telegram that was sent to Dr. Walvoord from Howard W. Ferrin who was the President of Providence Bible Institute on the day of Chafer's death on August 25, 1952:

> He finished his course with joy: a strong established seminary, a completed theology, a wide and fruitful public ministry are his legacy to the church of Christ for which we thank God; an inspiration to his colleagues and all true Christian leaders, one of whom Doctor Wilbur Smith is here with us today. We join in the expression of praise and in extending our heartfelt sympathy to all his dear ones.[8]

What an excellent summary of a life that was well spent for the glory of God.

---

[8] Chafer, *The Lewis Sperry Chafer Papers*.

Postlude

This book has evaluated Lewis Sperry Chafer's life, hermeneutics, theology, and contributions to dispensationalism. Chafer's background had significant impact on several aspects of his theology. His theology and life in turn had significant impact on the history of dispensationalism. This book has discussed four specific areas of impact in particular: his extensive writing, his unique systematization of dispensational truths, his mentoring of key figures in the movement, and his establishment of Dallas Theological Seminary.

The life and theology of Lewis Sperry Chafer should be emulated by dispensationalists instead of being dismissed in the interest of progression. There is more continuity in his theology with the essentialist dispensationalists as represented by Charles Ryrie than many are willing to acknowledge. However, there is a great deal of discontinuity between his teachings and those of the progressive dispensationalists. Additional research comparing several different representatives of classical, essentialist, and progressive dispensationalism is needed to further evaluate this trend.

Bibliography

"About DTS." http://www.dts.edu/about/stats/. Accessed 11 August 2006.

Baker, Bruce A. "Progressive Dispensationalism & Cessationism: Why They Are Incompatible." *Journal of Ministry and Theology* 8, no. 1 (Spring 2004): 53–88.

_____. "The Theological Method of Lewis Sperry Chafer." *Journal of Ministry and Theology* 5, no. 1 (Spring 2001): 29–69.

Blaising, Craig A., and Darrell L. Bock. *Progressive Dispensationalism.* Wheaton, IL: BridgePoint, 1993.

Bock, Darrell L. "Part 1: Evangelicals and the Use of the Old Testament in the New." *Bibliotheca Sacra,* 142, no. 567 (July–September 1985): 209–24.

_____. "Part 2: Evangelicals and the Use of the Old Testament in the New." *Bibliotheca Sacra* 142, no. 568 (October–December 1985): 306–19.

_____. "A Review of the Gospel According to Jesus." *Bibliotheca Sacra* 146, no. 581 (January – March 1989): 21–40.

———. "The Son of David and the Saints' Task: The Hermeneutics of Initial Fulfillment." *Bibliotheca Sacra* 150, no. 600 (October–December 1993): 440–57.

———. "Hermeneutics of Progressive Dispensationalism." In *Three Issues in Contemporary Dispensationalism*, ed. Herbert W. Bateman IV, 85–101. Grand Rapids, MI: Kregel, 1999.

Brumett, John. "Does Progressive Dispensationalism Teach a Posttribulational Rapture?—Part I." *Conservative Theological Journal* 2 (June 1998): 191–203.

———. "Does Progressive Dispensationalism Teach a Posttribulational Rapture?—Part II." *Conservative Theological Journal* 2 (September 1998): 319–32.

Chafer, Lewis Sperry. "An Introduction to the Study of Prophecy." *Bibliotheca Sacra* 100, no. 397 (January–March 1943): 98–134.

———. "Are There Two Ways to Be Saved?" *Bibliotheca Sacra* 105, no. 417 (January–March 1948): 1–2.

———. "Dispensationalism." *Bibliotheca Sacra* 93, no. 372 (October–December 1936): 390–449.

———. "Dr. C. I. Scofield." *Bibliotheca Sacra* 100, no. 397 (January–March 1943): 4–7.

_____. *He That Is Spiritual: A Classic Study of the Biblical Doctrine of Spirituality*. Rev. ed. Grand Rapids, MI: Zondervan Publishing House, 1967.

_____. *Major Bible Themes: 52 Vital Doctrines of the Scriptures Simplified and Explained*. Rev. John F. Walvoord. Rev. Ed. Grand Rapids, MI: Zondervan Publishing House, 1974.

_____. "Part 5: Bibliology." *Bibliotheca Sacra* 95, no. 378 (April – June 1938): 137–57.

_____. "Populating the Third Heaven." *Bibliotheca Sacra* 108, no. 430 (April–June 1951): 138–52.

_____. *Salvation*. Grand Rapids, MI: Kregel Publications, 1991.

_____. *Systematic Theology*. 8 vols. Grand Rapids, MI: Kregel Publications, 1993.

_____. *True Evangelism: Winning Souls by Prayer*. Grand Rapids, MI: Kregel Publications, 1993.

_____. *The Lewis Sperry Chafer Papers*. microform. Jamestown, NC: Schnappsburg University Press, 2002.

Essex, Keith H. "The Preparation and Contributions of Lewis Sperry Chafer." Th.M. thesis, Dallas Theological Seminary, 1974.

Green, Robert. "Lewis Sperry Chafer and Dallas Theological Seminary." TMs [electronic copy], 2004, Baptist Bible Seminary, Clarks Summit, PA.

Hannah, John D. "The Early Years of Lewis Sperry Chafer." *Bibliotheca Sacra* 144, no. 573 (January–March 1987): 3–24.

Houghton, George G. "Lewis Sperry Chafer, 1871–1952." *Bibliotheca Sacra* 128, no. 512 (October–December 1971): 291–300.

Lightner, Robert. "Progressive Dispensationalism." *Conservative Theological Journal* 4, no. 11 (April 2000): 46–64.

Lincoln, C. F. "Lewis Sperry Chafer." *Bibliotheca Sacra* 109, no. 436 (October–December 1952): 332–38.

MacArthur, John. *The Gospel According to Jesus: What Does Jesus Mean When He Says "Follow Me?"* Rev. and expanded ed. Grand Rapids, MI: Zondervan Publishing House, 1993.

Pate, C. Marvin. "A Progressive Dispensational View of Revelation." In *Four Views on the Book of Revelation*, ed. C. Marvin Pate, 133–175. Grand Rapids, MI: Zondervan Publishing House, 1998.

Ryrie, Charles Caldwell. *A Survey of Bible Doctrine*. Chicago, IL: Moody Press, 1995.

_____. *Basic Theology: A Popular Systemic Guide to Understanding Biblical Truth.* Chicago, IL.: Moody Press, 1999.

_____. "Covenant, New." In *The Wycliffe Bible Encyclopedia*, ed. Charles F. Pfeiffer, Howard Frederic Vos, and John Rea. Chicago, IL: Moody Press, 1975.

_____. *Dispensationalism.* Revised and Expanded ed. Chicago, IL.: Moody Press, 1995.

_____. *So Great Salvation: What It Means to Believe in Jesus Christ.* Wheaton, IL: Victor Books, 1989.

_____. *The Basis of the Premillennial Faith.* Dubuque, IA: ECS Ministries, 2005.

Sandy, D. Brent. *Plowshares & Pruning Hooks: Rethinking the Language of Biblical Prophecy and Apocalyptic.* Downers Grove, IL: InterVarsity Press, 2002.

Saucy, Robert L. *The Case for Progressive Dispensationalism: The Interface between Dispensational & Non-Dispensational Theology.* Grand Rapids, MI: Zondervan Publishing House, 1993.

Stallard, Mike. "An Essentialist Response to Robert A. Pyne's 'The New Man in an Immoral Society: Expectations between the Times.'" Paper presented at the annual meeting of the Evangelical Theological Society, San Jose, CA, 20–22 November 1991.

_____. "Émile Guers: An Early Darbyite Response to Irvingism and a Precursor to Charles Ryrie." *Conservative Theological Journal* 1, (April 1997): 31–46.

_____. "Literal Interpretation, Theological Method, and the Essence of Dispensationalism." *Journal of Ministry and Theology* 1, (Spring 1997): 6–37.

_____. "Prophetic Hope in the Writings of Arno C. Gaebelein: A Possible Demonstration of the Doxological Purpose of Biblical History." *Journal of Ministry and Theology* 2, (Fall 1998): 190–211.

_____. *The Early Twentieth-Century Dispensationalism of Arno C. Gaebelein.* Lewiston, NY: The Edwin Mellon Press, 2002.

Walvoord, John F. "A Review of Lewis Sperry Chafer's 'Systematic Theology.'" *Bibliotheca Sacra* 105, no. 417 (January–March 1948): 115–28.

_____. "A Review of Lewis Sperry Chafer's 'Systematic Theology' Fourth Edition." *Bibliotheca Sacra* 111, no. 442 (April–June 1954): 169.

Warfield, Benjamin B. "A Review of Lewis Sperry Chafer's 'He That Is Spiritual.'" *The Princeton Theological Review* Vol. XVII, (April 1919): 322.

Witmer, John A. "What Hath God Wrought, Fifty Years of Dallas Theological Seminary: Part I: God's Man and His Dream." *Bibliotheca Sacra* 130, no. 520 (October–December 1973): 291–305.

www.ingramcontent.com/pod-product-compliance
Lightning Source LLC
LaVergne TN
LVHW051522070426
835507LV00023B/3250